W9-AEW-246

Bill Barns
1974

THE RETURN
TO FAITH

Books by Clyde Reid

LET IT HAPPEN (With Jerry Kerns)
CELEBRATE THE TEMPORARY
GROUPS ALIVE, CHURCH ALIVE
THE EMPTY PULPIT
TWENTY-FIRST CENTURY MAN EMERGING
HELP! I'VE BEEN FIRED
THE GOD–EVADERS

Clyde Reid

THE RETURN
TO FAITH

Finding God in the Unconscious

ILLUSTRATED BY DAN MARSHALL

HARPER & ROW, PUBLISHERS
New York, Evanston, San Francisco, London

THE RETURN TO FAITH. Copyright © 1974 by Clyde H. Reid. All rights reserved. Printed in the United States of America. No part of this book may be used or reproduced in any manner whatsoever without written permission except in the case of brief quotations embodied in critical articles and reviews. For information address Harper & Row, Publishers, Inc., 10 East 53rd Street, New York, N.Y. 10022. Published simultaneously in Canada by Fitzhenry & Whiteside Limited, Toronto.

FIRST EDITION

Designed by C. Linda Dingler

Library of Congress Cataloging in Publication Data

Reid, Clyde H
    The return to faith; finding God in the unconscious.

    Includes bibliographical references.
    1. Experience (Religion)   2. Psychology, Religious.
I. Title.
BL53.R36   248   73–18426
ISBN 0–06–066822–9

ACKNOWLEDGEMENTS

Mandalas on pages 1, 17, 33, 89 by Miriam Argüelles from *Mandala,* copyright © 1972 by Shambala.

Photograph of the whole earth, page 57, courtesy NASA.

Photograph of vibrating steel disc, page 69, by Hans Peter Widner. From *Man and His Symbols*, edited by Carl Jung, copyright © by Aldus Books Ltd., London.

To my friend, CHARLES JOHNSTON
a teacher
who, in his own way, was God's man
because he gave of himself
and loved people

CONTENTS

PREFACE

I once had a fantasy in which I saw a strong man-figure straining and reaching toward the heavens where the hand of God awaited him. But the man was shackled to a large, heavy object like a huge stone that kept him from reaching his goal. The large, heavy object was in the shape of a church.

Man is steadily emerging into a new era of his existence, one in which he is turning back to reclaim the riches of his unconscious. He is growing out of the period of history in which he so feared his unconscious that he sealed it off and tried to live in his head. He is discovering some moments of wholeness by reuniting the incredible depths and riches of the unconscious with his intellectual gains. And he has rediscovered God, for God was there in the unconscious waiting for him. The implications of this rediscovery and this emerging wholeness for organized religion are deep.

We are ready to see that most of our religious structures were designed to fit man living in his head, cut off from his unconscious. This new man now demands a new style of religious expression. He wants a religion of consciousness, a religion that allows him to be both mind and body, both conscious and unconscious. That is what this book is about.

As we in the West enter a period of crisis with energy shortages and social problems, it will become increasingly crucial for religious leaders to help us enter an era of deeper inner strength. It will be more and more difficult for us to run away from our true selves with our fast automobiles, our fast pace of life, and our scramble for material riches. When we slow down of necessity, we will need the inner strength and peace with which we are currently strangers. Preaching will not get us there. Neither will mental gymnastics. A new approach to religion alone will suffice.

I woke up one morning in Zurich, Switzerland, with a sense of great energy. Two decisions were clear in my mind. I had to write this book, and I had to start my own center where I could try out some of the ideas and experiences for which I feel man is reaching. I was spending the spring studying at the C. G. Jung Institute in Zurich, and my analysis, my reading, and my reflections on the state of religion met or collided on the theme of an emerging religion of consciousness.

I want to thank my friends and teachers in Zurich, as well as Frau Hedda Baumann, the secretary-general of the Jung Institute, for their stimulation and help. Miss Andrea Dykes, Dr. Arnold Mindell, and Dr. Dieter Baumann were especially helpful and encouraging to me. Friends like Laura Dodson listened patiently to my ideas and helped convince me I was on an important track. My wife, Jennifer, read the manuscript and made many helpful suggestions, and Eleanor Hallowell did a beautiful job typing the manuscript as she had done earlier on my book, *Let It Happen*, written with Jerry Kerns. Helen and Frank Kampfe shared part of their summer and the hospitality of the Mackay Ranch in Montana, and this gave me more opportunity to write and test my ideas with loving friends. Jameson Jones, Iliff School of Theology president, helped make it possible for me to spend the spring at the Jung Institute, and I am grateful to him.

Denver, Colorado   CLYDE HENDERSON REID

THE RETURN
TO FAITH

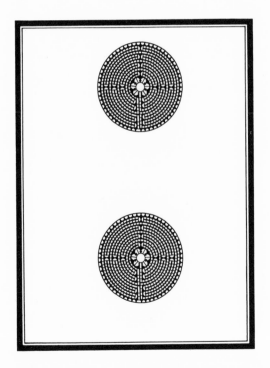

The labyrinth in Chartres Cathedral

1. THE MEANING OF FULL CONSCIOUSNESS

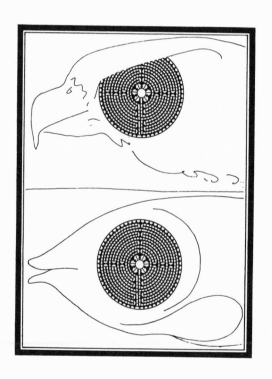

There is one enormous fact we need to face directly and honestly. The life of the spirit has very little to do with our churches, synagogues, and other institutions! The great religious teachings of the ages are true, far truer than we want them to be. Man is at his core a spiritual being. There is a God, known by many names and manifested in a million ways. This much has survived the onslaught of the scientific age: that religious realities persist and are *luminously true!*

Furthermore, the great religious truths are more desperately needed than ever before. We know from bitter experience that we have gained the whole world of material possessions, luxury living, and scientific achievement, yet lost our souls. There is a deep hunger for something more, for the life of the spirit without which man dies from within. And here is the sad paradox. Spiritual life is alive. Spirituality is everywhere. But spiritual vitality is not centered in, is not encouraged in, and is not flourishing in the churches.

Let me express this in more personal terms. I am a religious man. I know that deep within me there is that which goes beyond me, which connects me with the universe, with all humanity, with beauty and nature. It is essentially inexpressible, yet I call this transcendent dimension in me, God.

I believe in God. I feel, sense, experience his/her influence on my life in a thousand ways. I yearn for a deeper relationship with this God; I desire to celebrate his/her existence and mine! Part of the yearning is a desire occasionally to celebrate God's presence with others who feel as I do. So why don't I just go to church and do it, you may ask. Sing the great hymns, hear the prayers of the faithful, listen to the ancient words and rejoice! I wish it were that simple.

The problem is that I rarely find spiritual nourishment in churches and their rituals. And millions feel as I do. Literally dozens of books have been written in recent years about the problems of the modern church and why it has difficulty communicating with people. Hundreds of "renewal" programs have been launched to little avail. Still there is something missing, something wrong, something empty. I go to church and my spirit is not fed. I am bored more often than uplifted.

Is it not possible that we must finally face the unspeakable fact that God's Spirit has withdrawn from the churches? The vitality of the Holy Spirit is not often there! When we are honest, *much as we would prefer to believe otherwise,* we must admit that the power and vitality of God's Spirit is not often found in churches.

So what is the message in this momentous recognition? If the combined efforts of some of the Church's finest leaders have not been able to pump life into these dying institutions, should we not be asking what lies beyond? Where, then, is the Spirit to be found? What is the future shape of the religious life?

Answers and new directions are emerging, and I want to share some of my thoughts about them. My conclusions, though partial and tentative, grow out of my deep soul-searchings and my studies in psychology and religion. It is perhaps the world view of Carl Jung which has most influenced my thinking here, although I find reinforcement in many other streams of influence as well. These influences will be more obvious as I proceed. Let me state in capsule form the basic insight of the book, from which I can proceed in more detail.

It is very clear to me that what our world needs now is a new style of religious life! We need a new approach to religion that will let in new light, that will throw open the doors and windows and let the stale air of today's religion be replaced by the fresh wind of the spirit.

The style of religious life which predominates today appeals to us too often for the wrong reasons. It appeals to our hunger for social contact, but limits the contact too often to superficial pleasantries. It appeals to our need for approval. And so we go out of a sense of guilt and uneasiness, to be reassured that we are okay again by the clergy and by our fellow members. It deals with the religious life at a distance, *merely talking about religion.* But let someone begin to practice his or her religion and he is quickly put down as a fanatic or disturbed person. He isn't playing by the rules. You may feel I am being critical. That is not my purpose; criticism already abounds in printed form. My intention is to point to emerging alternatives.

I am proposing that we admit, allow, and honor a new approach to religious life that permits the wholeness of man to be involved, not just the top of his head and the seat of his pants. I am proposing that we seek a *religion of full consciousness,* not just the carefully monitored nicety of the rational, conscious self.

I am not proposing a new *religion.* That would be both foolish and ludicrous. It is an attitude toward religion and the religious life that I want to encourage, an attitude that can lead to deeper religious experience within churches or without, *wherever persons are open to allow it.* I am speaking to those who want their church life to be more deeply spiritual and vital, and I am speaking to those who are not fed by traditional religious approaches but are searching for that which feeds their spirits.

With a few notable exceptions, churches in general have not been open to such an attitude. Let us hope and pray that they may be more so, but let us wait for it no longer! Let us, for the sake of our souls, seek the religious life where we can find it.

A certain courage is required to pursue a religious style that is not the accepted pattern. But all movement in history requires persons with the courage to explore new frontiers. If you are so inclined, I invite you to ponder the issue with me further and seek to implement your own version of this call to a new style without guilt and without apology!

I am speaking of the need for a religion of full consciousness. To make sense of this expression, I must first, then, indicate what I mean by the term *full consciousness.*

Full Consciousness

To be fully conscious as a human being is to recognize and be in communication with both the conscious thoughts and the unconscious realities within. For example, I have within my unconscious some anger that does not belong to my individual historical existence. It was family anger I assimilated as a child, anger for being suddenly poor after the depression wiped out the family business. Being aware of that unconscious content means that I am less likely to misplace that anger on the wrong persons in inappropriate situations. Being aware of it makes it less dangerous but not harmless.

There are several other possibilities for handling that anger. I could simply behave angrily toward persons who mistreat me, aware as I do that I am angry at that time. Or I can be even more cut off from my feelings and my unconscious and behave angrily without being consciously aware that I am angry at anyone. The prototype for this behavior was the professor I once knew who slammed his fist down on the desk and shouted at the student quavering before him, "How do you dare suggest I'm angry?"

The truth is that we have an unconscious. The unconscious

has deep roots, memories, forgotten traumas, as well as primitive shadow dimensions that we moderns try to forget and suppress. The unconscious also has deep riches to offer us—peace, beauty, depth, strength, help, and light. God is there. Of these riches I shall have more to say later.

The wholeness of the human psyche, then, includes not only the conscious reason and awareness but the dark, scary realities and positive, enriching contents of the unconscious as well. Anyone willing to take an hour to discuss his dreams or to experiment with meditation can get in touch with these unconscious realities. Most modern psychology is based on the reality of the unconscious and its power to influence our behavior with or without our conscious awareness. The task is to enhance the positive aspects of the unconscious and to resist the negative impulses that oppose our wholeness.

Perfect wholeness is of course not possible. We will never be *totally* aware of our unconscious. It is much too vast. But we can establish a healthy, cooperative relationship between our consciousness and our unconscious. This is the goal of human existence, the wholeness toward which we strive. This goal will make more sense against the historical background of human consciousness, as it has been explored by scholars.[1]

In the beginning man had no distinct self-consciousness. His consciousness and his unconscious were one, indissolubly bound up together. So primitive man felt a oneness with nature, with plants and animals. To him they were all part of the living unity of the world. Neumann puts it this way:

The essential fate of man, at least of the mature modern man, is enacted on three fronts which, although interconnected, are nonetheless clearly marked off from one another. The world as the outside

1. My very condensed summary is based on Jungian thought in general, but is indebted specifically to the very important work by Erich Neumann, *The Origins and History of Consciousness* (New York: Pantheon Books, 1954).

world of extrahuman events, the community as the sphere of interhuman relationships, the psyche as the world of interior human experience—these are the three basic factors which govern human life, and man's creative encounter with each of them is decisive for the development of the individual. In the initial stage, however, these territories have not yet become separated from one another, neither man from the world, nor individual from the group, nor ego consciousness from the unconscious.[2]

All the social, religious, and historical evidence points to the late birth of the individual from the collective and from the unconscious.[3]

The primitive had no problem of being out of touch with his unconscious. He was his unconscious, living directly and intuitively. But man could not remain in an undifferentiated, simple state. He was called to become something more; he had an intention to live out, a destiny.

Emergence of the Ego

The next stage in man's maturing is the emergence of the ego out of unconsciousness into consciousness. In its historical beginnings, Neumann points out, consciousness would rise then fall back. The emergence of the ego into consciousness requires libido, energy, and so the primitive would soon tire of conscious activity and become drowsy. This tendency for the unconscious to pull the infant conscious ego back into itself creates a conflict, a tension between the two.

Slowly then, man's conscious ego emerged, pulling itself out of the unity with the unconscious. The conscious ego became more and more aware, more and more complex and differentiated, more and more out of touch with the unconscious. The functions of thinking and feeling emerged, following the perceptive functions of sensation and intuition. The contents of the

2. Neumann, op. cit., p. 267.
3. Ibid., p. 270.

unconscious continued to exert a powerful influence on the activity of the conscious ego in spite of their separation.

To the emerging ego the unconscious thus appeared as potentially destructive. Mythologically, it was the Great Mother waiting in the wings to devour the infant ego. Neumann has explored the history of human myths in his impressive work on consciousness, and has demonstrated the parallel myths from many cultures that support the psychological evidence on the emergence of man's consciousness.

Neumann says of the tendency of the unconscious to destroy consciousness: "This is identical with the basic fact that ego consciousness has to wrest libido from the unconscious for its own existence, for, unless it does so, its specific achievement falls back into the unconscious, in other words is 'devoured.' "[4] It is a natural consequence that modern man still lives in fear of his own unconscious, often tending to ignore it, deny its existence, and treat it as an enemy. These fears derive from the earlier, adolescent stage in man's conscious development when the unconscious was indeed the enemy of consciousness. But as Neumann also points out:

Later, when the personality feels itself allied not only to the ego but to the whole, consciousness no longer sees itself threatened to the degree that the adolescent ego was, and the unconscious now presents other aspects than those of danger and destruction.[5]

The emergence of consciousness in man is a very complicated story, and the serious scholar is referred to the work of Neumann and others. I am aware of the danger of oversimplifying, but I want to sketch a few features of the continuing evolution of consciousness in order to consider their implications for religion.

As man became more conscious and his rational side more

4. Neumann, op. cit., p. 299.
5. Ibid.

and more highly developed, he tried to leave his unconscious behind. But in the mature person there is yet another task for the second half of life: a return to claim the richness of the unconscious for his spiritual growth and development. Historically, we are just entering this phase with the emergence of depth psychology as a parallel. The mature person does not live in his rational, conscious ego alone. In the unconscious there is his deeper self, waiting to help unite conscious ego and unconscious contents. If he ignores this task, something goes sour.

But as the ego emerged, the result was a split between conscious and unconscious that left man incomplete. This dangerous schism, Neumann says, is reflected in the cultural crisis of our time and is expressed in overintellectualization. We all know persons who live "in their heads," and millions of us do this to a large extent. The person living in his head, in his rational world of concepts, is often unaware of the important messages of his body, his senses, and his intuition. He does not know when he is angry or when he is loving, when he is afraid or when he is strong. He is dangerously cut off from an important part of who and what he is: a physical being. He has left his physical self behind, often believing that the body is evil, the mind sublime.

I remember one theologian who was asked in the course of an awareness exercise to look at the bodies of the persons around him. He later exclaimed, "I have always looked at people's heads. I didn't even know they had bodies!" When consciousness becomes so removed from the unconscious that we lose touch with our bodies, we discover to our dismay that we have left behind an enormously important warehouse of tools and equipment that we need to survive.[6] If the conscious

6. Much frontier psychology today is working to help people rediscover their bodily awareness, so its rich resources may work with them rather than against them. Gestalt therapy and Alexander Lowen's bioenergetic analysis are among these. See James

ego loses all touch with the unconscious, then the unconscious may erupt in disastrous ways, evidenced collectively in the inhuman wars that have plagued this time.

Reclaiming the Unconscious

The great task for modern man is to turn back toward his unconscious and make friends with it. The unconscious has contents we prefer to ignore because they upset us. They may be ugly, earthy, nasty, or embarrassing. We try to live an unreal existence, acting as if the ugly shadow realities were not part of us. But it does not work well. We are not complete. To find our real selves we must reclaim the unconscious, come to terms with it, struggle with it, and use its tremendous energy in our movement toward wholeness and psychic fullness. For not only are there ugly contents and primitive contents in our depths, but also the secret of the soul, the power of God. Neumann puts it: "The turning of the mind from the conscious to the unconscious, the responsible *rapprochement* of human consciousness with the powers of the collective psyche, that is the task of the future."[7]

These basic stages in man's development may be pictured as follows:

In Figure A there is no ego; there is only the intuitive, primitive unconscious. In Figure B the ego has emerged; man tends to live in his conscious, intellectual self, keeping a tight lid on the dangerous contents of the unconscious, which he fears will upset his hold on reality. In spite of the boundary between the conscious and unconscious, occasional eruptions break

---

Lynwood Walker's treatment of this important unity: *Body and Soul: Gestalt Therapy and Religious Experience* (Nashville: Abingdon Press, 1971).

7. Neumann, op, cit., p. 393.

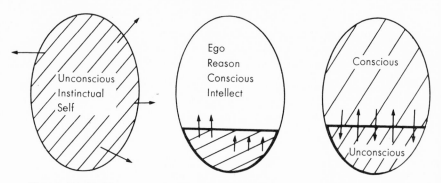

Figure A: Primitive Man   Figure B: Western Man   Figure C: Emerging Man

through. The eruptions may upset our lives, but they may also be psychic events, flashes of intuition or other indications of the richness of the unconscious. In Figure C, the emerging situation, man turns back to reclaim both his shadow side and the immense riches of the unconscious, keeping a more porous communication open with that dimension of himself, but retaining the gains of the conscious ego and enlarging it.

Because the style of our culture ignores the scary contents of the unconscious, a tremendous amount of mental illness and fear and suffering has resulted. But when we look these contents square in the eye and discover also our resources for dealing with them, they are not nearly so scary.

I would like to list some of the contents of the unconscious that I have discovered in myself or seen at first hand in persons with whom I have worked in groups. It will of necessity be a partial list, for the unconscious is vast and unfathomable.

Some Contents of the Unconscious

Intuition: a knowing that is not rationally discovered

Sexuality

Violence

The desire for love and tenderness
The tendency to use others for one's own purposes
Extrasensory powers
Growth impulses
Possession by others, living or dead
Fearful fantasies: monsters, dragons, witches
Leadings and guidance: a deep inner wisdom (the inner Self)
God

All of these dimensions and many, many more are in us and need the light of day. When we pretend they are not really part of us, the possibility of their becoming dangerous is greatly increased. To ignore even the positive contents of the unconscious can be dangerous. For example, to ignore our growth impulses stifles those impulses and turns them sour so they work against us. To admit their presence in us as powerful psychic realities is scary but freeing, their power to control us being diminished by their becoming known.

Two examples of these unconscious contents from my own experience may make them clearer. I recently had a vivid experience of intuition that surprised me in its clarity and quality. I was working with a proud young woman in a group. She had presented several concerns that she wanted to resolve, but no clear answer had emerged as to how she could grow in respect to them. Neither I nor the group had discovered the key to help her open any doors.

Suddenly, I had the strong impulse to hold the young woman in my lap. I did an instant check with myself: "Are you thinking of this because she is an attractive young woman and you would enjoy holding her?" If the answer had been yes, I would have kept quiet. But my feeling was that this was an inner impulse I should trust and honor. So I said to her, "I want to ask you to try something. Would you let me hold you in my lap?"

She hesitated, then replied, "I'd feel silly." She went on, "But I'd rather be held." For the next ten minutes or so I held this grown woman in my lap as a child. She cuddled up like a three year old and clung tightly. After a few minutes she said quietly, "My daddy never held me in his lap." And later, in reviewing the experience, she made this revealing comment: "Maybe if I could allow myself to be held and loved more easily, I wouldn't have to hate so much."

Intuitive leaps such as this become possible and can help others to significant growth if we trust the intuition and test it. Had I been more uncertain of my own motives, or had I been more afraid to risk, she would not have broken through to the deep inner need to be held and realized its importance in her life.

The second example concerns a young woman in a group with which I was working. She presented herself as a fearful, quiet person who avoided feelings and lived very much in her head. We asked her about this one day in a group session. She told us that she had had a lot of fear as a child. She was terrified of the closet in her bedroom, certain there were monsters inside but too frightened to get up and look.

I asked her if she would like to get rid of the monsters in her closet, the group and I offering to help her do so. The monsters were psychic realities still influencing her adult behavior. She said she was afraid to do so, but she would try. I asked her to imagine that closet door. I said that I was at her side and that she could open the door if she wanted to. She almost did, but reported that she was too frightened. I simply told her that when she was ready to do so, we were ready to help her.

Several weeks later a member of the group asked the young woman about her closet. "Oh," she said, "my husband helped me with that the other day and I opened the closet door. I found a short, fat green monster sitting in the corner of the closet. I told him to get out, but he just shrank back in farther. Finally, I got in and pushed him out. He's not there anymore." She also reported that she had been allowing herself to feel more. She and her husband had had their first fight in over a year of marriage. Previously, she had always denied that she was angry so there was no way he could fight with her. She felt good that she could allow herself the freedom to be honest about her feelings.

In many such instances the individuals are not sufficiently distressed to seek the help of a psychiatrist or psychologist. They do not appear to need therapy; through an experience in a growth group with trained leadership, however, they are able to open some doors into the unconscious, which means more joy in their lives and more freedom to be themselves. When fear of the unconscious prevails, growth is less possible.

* * *

The question now arises, "So what does this history of consciousness issue have to do with religion?" That question is the heart of this book. I feel the two issues are intimately, indissolubly related, and I hope to indicate why I believe so. It is my conviction that most religious institutions are designed to fit an immature stage of man's development. Most religion is designed for conscious man who has rejected his unconscious but who has not yet returned to find his unity with that interior self. This is perhaps the deeper meaning of the word *repentance,* literally a turning back. It is time to repent and discover religious styles that will reclaim man's unity with his neglected and rejected unconscious: religion for the whole man, fully conscious.

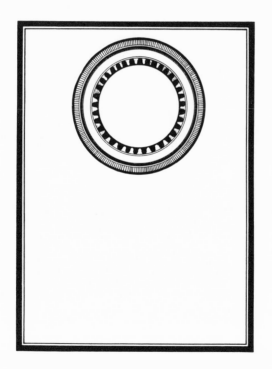

An image of the mantra OM

2. THE WORLD IS BECOMING THE CHURCH

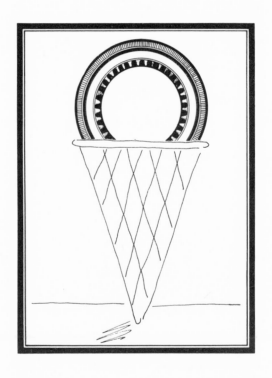

The men of a particular village once found a huge, elegant, beautiful elephant wandering near their village. They were so impressed, they decided to capture the elephant so others could see it as well. They feared no one would believe them otherwise. And so they captured the lovely beast and put it in a big tent. So many people came from near and far to see the giant elephant that the tent was badly overcrowded.

The men of the village conferred together and decided to build a temple around the tent, keeping the people away from the elephant to protect it. But the people jammed into the temple so that it was hard to breathe. Inside the tent, the elephant lay down and died. Before she died, however, the giant animal gave birth to quintuplets. The babies escaped by crawling out from under the tent and running around loose in the world.

When the villagers found their elephant had died, and some of the elephant worshipers in the temple asked why it didn't get up, they denied it was dead. They had too many printed programs prepared in advance, the offerings were too lucrative, and the paid elephant keepers who took care of the temple didn't want to lose their jobs. They even built an addition to the temple and made it an elephant museum and library. There was talk of developing a school of elephant studies in the village.

Meanwhile, the dead elephant inside its tent began to smell bad, and occasionally an elephant devotee would ask the elephant keepers, "Are you sure the elephant is alive? Are you sure there's a real elephant in there?" The elephant keepers assured the people the elephant was real.

Reports began to reach the temple that young live elephants had been seen here and there around the countryside outside the temple and its village. "Nonsense!" they replied. "Rumors!" "Everyone knows the only real elephant is the one in our temple." And for a time the people were satisfied, for they continued to come to the temple, hoping for a glimpse of the one, true elephant.

*   *   *

At a critical point in my life I attended a five-day workshop on personal growth led by a man with impressive credentials. He was not only a doctor of medicine, but a research psychiatrist at the University of California as well and an authority on Gestalt therapy. Those five days helped me make a critically important change in my life. The fascinating thing about the workshop was that the leader not only used Gestalt and encounter methods, but also led us in a series of meditation experiences.

In the encounter sessions I got in touch with some of my weaknesses and my need for change. But the meditation helped me correlate and integrate my strengths and move in new directions. The leader spoke about God without apology and led us to experience our deep inner resources, God among them.

On the surface it seems rather strange for a "religious" leader to learn meditation and find an experience of God under the guidance of a research psychiatrist! But that is precisely what happened. Dr. Claudio Naranjo, who led the workshop, is not only a psychiatrist but an authority on the psychology of meditation. I found him a deeply spiritual man. My experience in his workshop is a symbol of the religious situation today. The world is becoming the Church, while many churches cling to the past and resist religious depth.

Consider some strange facts illustrative of this topsy-turvy situation. I was not taught meditation in my theological school. To my knowledge it is not taught in most seminaries. Prayer and meditation are treated intellectually and described rationally, but no one sits down and leads theological students in the techniques of meditation. Most of the faculty are suspicious of it and have never taken time to expose themselves to meditation and learn what it really is about. They look down on such concerns and convey that attitude to their students. Yet meditation is a powerful tool for the spiritual life and an important avenue to the presence of God.

Our theological schools are still for the most part trying to train rational Western man, who deals with the world through his head, by means of ideas and concepts. To learn meditation a student at a typical theological school must watch the corner drug store for a poster announcing meditation classes offered by one of the esoteric cult groups in that neighborhood. The world is becoming the Church, while the Church lives in a rational world of scholarship cut off from the deeper spiritual currents alive in the world today. Is it small wonder that our clergy are ill prepared to relate to the more vital persons in our culture?

One of the most fascinating centers in America is the Esalen Institute, with programs in San Francisco and in Big Sur, California. The Esalen catalog announces: "Esalen Institute is a center to explore those trends in education, religion, philosophy and the physical and behavioral sciences which emphasize the potentialities and values of human existence."

One can find more vitality and willingness to explore man's spiritual life through programs offered by Esalen than by anything available within the churches today. Three samples from the Esalen catalog follow:

One workshop, "Gestalt and Spiritual Practice," is descripted as "one of a series of programs relating Gestalt awareness practice to the spiritual disciplines developed within (and sometimes in opposition to) the great world religions."

Another workshop is "Psychosynthesis: A Return to Center." The information refers to the calm center within us as "a point of compassionate perspective where we can tap into sources of integrative energy and wisdom." Methods employed in this program include guided imagery, gestalt, symbolic art work, movement, journal writing, and meditation.

Another program offered on the same page as the two mentioned above is entitled "New Paths to Healing" and is led by a medical doctor trained in acupuncture, internal medicine and cardiology, Gestalt psychology, Reichian energetics and structural integration. The catalog continues: "He is currently interested in fusing the above teachings toward developing a humanistic model for healing the whole person (body-mind-spirit)."

Here is God at work in the world. Here is the world becoming the church, the place where God can be found and where his/her activity can be felt.

I would like to share some additional experiences that I feel add documentation to my claim that the world is becoming the Church. Not long ago the Association for Humanistic Psychology had its annual meeting at Squaw Valley, California. Many of the psychologists, therapists, and educators who belong to this organization affirm the transcendent dimension in man and see its important implications for man's health and growth. As I attended one workshop after another, I was struck with the heavy emphasis on various forms and techniques drawn from Buddhism, Sufism, Taoism, yoga, and Hopi rituals. I saw psychoanalysts led in a variety of meditation styles drawn from the world's great religions and finding deep meaning in those styles. Religion and psychology are converging in some exciting ways.

I had been asked to chair a "religion section meeting" to bring together some of the participants who wished to explore the relationship between religion and humanistic psychology. A small group of us met for an hour or so in the evening. After some discussion one member of the group suggested that we sit together in silence in the nearby chapel, and the entire group agreed. What followed was a very simple but moving experience. We sat in silence in the dimly lighted chapel. One member of the group moved to the organ console and played a few very simple chords. I felt my spirit lifted and a deep sense of contact with those who shared the experience. We had stopped talking about religion and opened ourselves to an experience which was for me religious. We came from a variety of backgrounds, but felt our oneness as human beings. We left quietly as we felt ready to go. The world is becoming the Church!

I am quite aware that such an experience would not qualify as a "religious" experience for many persons. They would ask questions such as:

What was the theological content of such an event?

In what sense could this event possibly qualify to be referred to as "the church"?

Where are the qualified leaders?

Where are the safeguards against theological error?

So what do I mean when I say the world is becoming the Church? First, I do not mean that people in the world are joining the churches, or that they are now open to the idea of membership in a particular church or synagogue. I do mean that I find spiritual vitality in many places outside the churches, often unlikely places such as psychological conferences. I find persons concerned with their spiritual growth, and open to experiences that put them in touch with transcendent realities. In this sense the world is becoming the Church, the place where we find the presence of God, where we get in touch with spiritual vitality. The spirit of God is free in the world, appearing anywhere and everywhere, inspiring reverence and awe, calling us to look beyond the narrow confines of our lives, to get in touch with the deep resources of beauty, peace, and strength within us.

Another experience from my Squaw Valley time strengthens this conviction. On our final day at the conference my wife and I got up early to play tennis before breakfast. It was a crisp fall morning with the sun just coming up. As we enjoyed our tennis game, we could see a large group of perhaps forty persons sitting on the grass nearby, meditating and chanting. The current image of the modern psychologist hardly fits this picture.

I find this "outside the church" interest in religious life almost everywhere I turn. I see classes in transcendental meditation offered in a small Montana town, and in virtually every corner of the nation. I find yoga classes and yoga literature available almost everywhere I go. Thousands flock to hear a guru, looking for a spiritual guide, a teacher they can trust and believe.

As I spent three and a half months at the Jung Institute in Switzerland, I found many persons deeply interested and concerned with spiritual life. Their studies in Jungian psychology and their self-explorations led them to a natural awareness of the life of the spirit. Many of them did not express that interest through church involvement, but I found it refreshing that their lives reflected a deep concern for their relationship with the transcendent and spiritual dimension of life. They did not question its reality, because they had experienced it from within.

I am increasingly convinced that when human beings look into their unconscious, look deeply within themselves, they find God. They may not use that terminology. They may not find church rituals meaningful. They may not express that religious interest by joining groups or churches, but they are living out of a spiritual orientation. They have a way of looking at life and experiencing life that includes the existence of God and his/her direction in the world. They live their religion, though they may not *belong* to *a* religion.

As Claudio Naranjo has written:

One might even say that today the broad cultural divisions of religion, art, reason, standards of morality, and political institutions are "dead"; at least this is how they are now being experienced by a growing number of people. They are left behind, as a snake leaves behind its old skin, unchanged and still beautiful perhaps, but too tight, and therefore not functional. . . . Even if God is "dead" in the Western church, he is still alive in the experience of individuals who do not invoke his name. . . . But although formal religion may be dead, the source of its forms is closer than ever to man.[1]

The world is becoming the Church! People are discovering God (though they may not invoke that name) through their work with psychiatrists, through meditation in a yoga class in the local gymnasium, through encounter groups, and in many other ways. Persons who have experienced LSD trips have often reported that their deep inner exploration while under the influence of the drug has been a deeply religious experience. While the danger of using LSD is clearly established, and while the risk may outweigh the spiritual benefits, it remains true that many have emerged from their LSD experience open to the reality of God in their lives for the first time. Many of these experiences affirm that God is in our unconscious. Whether we contact our unconscious by way of meditation, examination of dreams, or by means of a powerful drug, God is present there. Our task is to learn the most fruitful and therapeutic ways we can help others find God within.

In my experience I believe we find God in four basic ways: through external authority, through relationships with other living persons, by means of internal messages, and through

1. *The One Quest* (New York: The Viking Press, 1972), pp. 4, 11.

numinous experiences. The following outline may help to make clear my meaning:

HOW PERSONS FIND GOD

I.   Through External Authority
     Bible reading
     Other books
     Speeches and sermons
     The Church
     Experiences in nature

II. Through Relationships with Persons
     Therapeutic relationships
     Personal friends
     Intensive groups
     Large groups (as religious fellowships)

III. Internal Messages
     Dreams
     Convictions
     Meditations or fantasies

IV. Numinous Experiences
     Visions, voices, etc. (as the appearance of Jesus, Mary, etc.)

Many people come to a deep life-changing conviction about God and his/her role in their lives through reading a Bible passage or a book that grasps them deeply. This is probably a rational process for the most part—finding an idea or concept that seems to have unusual power. I remember the words of Paul in the New Testament: "God . . . himself gives to all men life and breath and everything" (Acts 17:25, RSV). The words have had deep meaning in my own life.

Some people seem to relate to the Church as an ancient and traditional institution, accepting its authority over their lives as a living relationship. They are finding God through an external authority, in contrast with others who relate to a specific group of persons in a *particular* local church and find God through that relationship with particular people.

For many persons the most religious time in their lives is when they are standing on the ocean shore or in the mountains or in a garden, relating to God as expressed in the beauty and mystery of nature. Again, nature becomes an external authority for God's presence and activity, even though experienced inwardly as a feeling of awe and relationship with the earth. It is, of course, very difficult to separate what is external authority and what is internal feeling, and my categories are artificial in that sense.

I know many persons who have felt or experienced God through other persons. A deep relationship with another human being is a miracle in itself. Communication is a miracle when it occurs, and communication with another person can be felt as a religious experience. The meeting of minds and spirits can be powerful and life-changing. For this reason, since the beginning of the human relations movement and its use of intensive group experiences to foster human understanding, people have reported their group experiences as the most deeply religious experiences of their lives.

Finding God through relationships may take place in the office of a psychiatrist, or over a cup of coffee when two friends share deeply of their lives and feelings with each other. It may be in an encounter group where one can find acceptance, love, and forgiveness, or it may be in a church fellowship. The ancient words, "Where love is, there God is also," have deep significance.

People also experience God from within, as I have discussed in some detail already. Dreams and fantasies may offer symbols of God's presence that have great impact. In various meditation experiences one can experience this same contact with the unconscious and find God there. Another "internal" way to find

God is through the feelings. I have at times had a deep conviction that I was to follow a particular path, and that it was God's will I do so.

While many misled psychologists have tried to label numinous experiences as an expression of illness or insanity, it remains true that normal, healthy people sometimes experience visions. I have friends who have had visions or numinous experiences that convinced them of God's presence. While some authorities have difficulty believing such experiences because they are not rational or "scientific," I cannot dismiss them so easily. I have seen positive fruits in the lives of their beholders, and I believe in taking them seriously.

I remember the young theology student in one of my classes who had such a numinous experience. One day he told us with great joy of an unusual experience that had happened the night before. I share this with his permission:

I went to the church where I work and went to my office. No one was around. I was kinda angry and distressed. I was not fully in touch with myself, and I was trying to get in touch with my feelings. As I sat in my office, I thought I heard a voice saying, "I called you to come to the sanctuary, not to your office." I ignored the voice at first, thinking perhaps I had imagined it. But it came again, and this time I obeyed and went to the sanctuary.

As I entered, I looked toward the cross hanging above the altar. I had the distinct feeling, "I'm not worthy to be here. Forgive me, Lord, I am a sinner." I couldn't look toward that cross, and I spun around. At the rear of the sanctuary is a white statue, a figure of Christ carrying the cross on his shoulder and wearing a crown of thorns. I felt I had no place to hide. Something crumbled me to my knees. Tears came and then I felt as if someone were lifting me up to my feet and gently shoving me toward the altar. I resisted and hung onto the pews, but I experienced hard shoves, as a force behind me.

Then it was as though a hand had struck me in the back and I was flattened prone on the altar steps. The feeling kept coming, "I'm not good enough to be here; I'm not good enough to be a minister . . ." Again, I felt picked up and moved forward. I became very angry at God for some of the things that had happened in my life, my mother's sudden death and other things. I let these angry feelings come out and pounded the floor with my fists.

Again, I felt lifted to my feet and toward the altar, where I had to read the open Bible there. It was Psalm 24, and I found the words comforting. I felt good, released, and resurrected. I was free to leave, and going down the aisle, I had an entirely different feeling as I looked at that statue of Jesus.[2]

John's back was still sore the next day. Months later the experience was still helping him to feel okay about himself.

Many people have such experiences, yet do not share them or honor them for fear of being thought crazy or being misunderstood. Yet they represent one of the ways in which God reaches us through our unconscious. The experience of Jesus or Mary or some other figure in a numinous vision may be dramatic and have deep influence on the person's life. Such reports are too common and pervading to disregard them as expressions of insanity or imbalance.

So we find a variety of ways in which men experience God. I have listed only those with which I have some personal familiarity. There are many others, to be sure. Through the centuries the Christian Church has been suspicious of men finding God in some of the ways mentioned, because those modes were not subject to the authority of its leaders. The Church has always been leary of God's activity outside its own walls. The Church has been jealous of its own authority, preferring to have God under control, available to the people only when announced and controlled by the clergy. While this seems

2. Material used with permission of Stephen John Farquhar.

ridiculous, it sums up much of the history of the Church. Bloody massacres and persecutions have been carried out to protect that right of the Church to say when and where God may appear and in what way God's favor may be dispensed.

So it is time today to set aside the Church's claims to have God in a little box. God is and always has been free in the world. He/she appears to people or speaks to them or communicates to them in myriad ways, none of them controlled by religious institutions. And it is becoming increasingly apparent that God's spirit is free in the world. Where there is human vitality and creativity, he/she is there. Where the action is, defending human rights against big business or big politics, there God is. The world is God's arena and Church.

We are now ready for a new definition of what it means to be a religious person, a new definition of piety. Under the old definition, a pious person was one who

(1) accepted a body of cherished dogma;
(2) attended the ritual observances in a specific location regularly and faithfully;
(3) contributed financially to maintain the physical structures, the paid staff, and the program at that location; and
(4) demonstrated the "moral life" by being "nice" to those attending the same local fellowship. (Immoral behavior in one's business, private relations, or wartime activities are acceptable.)

Being a religious person really has little to do with those old criteria. Being religious has to do with the recognition of God in one's life and spirit. It has to do with how one spends one's time, money, and energy. It has to do with honesty and justice and following one's destiny. It has to do with the sharing of the self with others, the sharing of energy and love and concern. We have made religion and the religious life an institutional business, and somehow we have missed the mark.

I find it exciting and beautiful that the world is becoming the Church. I rejoice that God is active everywhere. I do not care that God comes in many guises, under many names, and in different ways to different people. I know that this is one world, and it is God's.

The emergence of a new religious style has deep implications for the future of man. There are new directions emerging within the existing religious institutions that can bring new life to religious fellowships. For persons whose loyalties remain with the religious organizations, these new directions bring new hope for revitalized churches. At the same time, for the millions who no longer find church life meaningful, the new religious style opens the possibility of a meaningful religious life without the necessity of affiliating with the traditional religions.

Religion of full consciousness is possible because man is reclaiming his unconscious, claiming it for his own, reuniting consciousness and unconscious as allies—an auspicious evolutionary movement. I will now discuss some of the myths we carry in our beings and in our culture and which serve as formidable barriers to this new religion of consciousness.

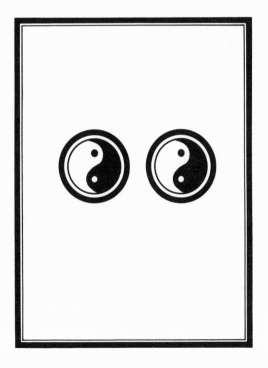

Ying-yang symbol of man
and woman, birth and death

3. SOME MYTHS THAT MUST DIE

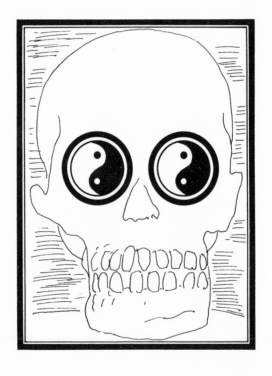

If it is true that God's spirit is free in the world, and if it is true that man is reclaiming his unconscious, it is clear that we need new religious forms and styles to fit this new human situation. Such forms and styles as I see emerging will be discussed in my concluding chapters. There are, however, many barriers within us as human beings that resist this newness, particularly the many myths to which we hold tenaciously. Some of the more prominent ones demand scrutiny.

We live by myths. And myths can be very important and very useful. Take, for example, the myth that kings rule by divine will and guidance. This was a very useful myth for centuries and was very widespread. It allowed national loyalties to emerge that brought people together into cooperating societies rather than warring tribes. It made more possible the emergence of legal systems with focused power to enforce laws for the common good. The myth, however, has outlived its usefulness, lingering on with a strong hook in our emotions but basically nonfunctional. With the abuses of the myth finally outweighing its advantages, it can now be seen as a myth and not as an eternal law of nature.

Similarly, there are some Christian myths that have outlived their usefulness. Since they have begun to die or decline, their continuing existence becomes more and more an embarrassment, a dead weight anchoring us to the past. It is time to become self-conscious about these unnecessary burdens and the effect they have in our daily lives.

Among the many myths that must die, there are seven that I feel prevent us or hinder us from moving to a religion of full consciousness. (1) *The exclusiveness myth* is the idea of one and only one true way, one true religion, one door to heaven. (2) *The either-or myth,* our inheritance from primitive thought, has led us to separate the world into good and bad, right and wrong, black and white. Its tragic consequences have left their ugly mark long enough. (3) *The holy man myth* views the clergy as having special access to God and his/her Truth. This myth has led us to an educated clergy and a laity willing to leave religious matters to the ordained holy men (and a few women). (4) *The dependency myth* forces us to find someone, some group, some system with the right answers so we can put our utter, blind faith in them and be saved. Religious torpor and the charlatanism in the name of religion are the outcome. (5) *The original sin myth,* an unfortunate misreading of God's creation, has been politically useful but destructive of human spirits. (6) *The nice guy myth,* which has led to great phoniness among Christians, conveys the idea that a "good" person never hurts anyone, is always sweet and kind and thinks no ugly thoughts. It denies the unconscious, leaving us prey to dishonesty and hypocrisy. (7) *The morality myth* is the idea of a code of perfect conduct for the "religious" person to follow. This has resulted in moralistic thinking and behavior, causing us to miss the leading of truly moral instincts. Each of these modern myths will be discussed in more detail.

The Exclusiveness Myth

A commonplace Christian doctrine holds the Christian way to be the one true religion. All other religions of the world are simply mistaken distortions of the truth. Christians have therefore looked down upon their poor misled neighbors as pagans, infidels, ignorant people who should know better but do not. This ugly doctrine, often couched in more polite language meant to tone down the unpalatable blatancy of its meaning, no longer fits the realities of this world as we know it.

I speak of Christianity as one who follows Christ as his leader and example. Christ made a life-changing difference to me. I honor him and revere his teachings. But I cannot believe he would have me close my eyes to the deep spiritual truths in other religions. I cannot believe he would have me reject spiritual fellowship with those who follow another prophet. For if there is one message in the Bible, it is that we are one human race under one God. Those religious teachers who claim that all of us should follow *their* path because all other paths are wrong simply proclaim their own narrowness. They seek power rather than truth.

I have experienced the spiritual richness in this world apart from strictly Christian institutions and teachings. Some of the most deeply spiritual persons I have met have not been Christians. Some have been Zen Buddhists, some Hindu, some with no label at all. In some, not all, of the best-known Christian leaders, on the other hand, one finds a rigidity, a disinterest in persons, a hunger for power that hardly proclaims their spiritual depth.

The exclusiveness myth is divisive and vicious, preventing us from really listening to the truth in our neighbor. It keeps us locked in our silly religious tower, cut off from dialogue with the world that would enrich our spirits. *There is no one true religious way.* As tremendously true and important as Jesus' way is, it is not the only way to God!

In my own life I have discovered the rich, deep beauty and peace of the spiritual realm of life through meditation taught by followers of many traditions. I have been profoundly impressed by religious teachings from Sufi wisdom, Hopi rituals, and primitive societies. This does not mean I am not a Christian. I am most fully a Christian when I seek truth with all my heart and soul and mind and strength. And I find hundreds of persons who can say what I have just said: that their lives are enriched by many and varied streams of religious thought and practice. To close yourself off to only Christian sources is to limit and narrow your life experience.

Our continued proclamation of this Christian arrogance that we have the one true way is divisive. We risk not being taken seriously with the truth and insight we do have to share. Those of us in differing religious traditions have much to learn from each other. It is really sad when someone wants only to teach you his way and does not understand that he has much to learn from you as well.

The Christian doctrine of exclusive truth, exclusive access to heaven and eternal life, is nonsense. That is not the way the world is. It is time to give it up as mistaken zeal and see the world as filled with God's truth and presence, expressed in many differing cultural garments, even if we feel that *for us* the primary path is that of Christ. For someone else the primary path may be that of Buddhism, and that individual may be far more advanced spiritually than we. So why should we not learn from him or her?

The exclusiveness myth is born out of insecurity and does not belong in the religious life. When we are not sure of ourselves, we shout to let everyone (and ourselves) know how sure we are. It only reveals an insecurity about our religious position when we must convince others they are wrong. Such a self-defeating and alienating policy should now be given up.

The Either-Or Myth

More pernicious and more pervading is the dualism or either-or myth, the great mother-myth of the exclusiveness just discussed. This very ancient idea divides the world into opposites. Things are good or they are bad. They are black or they are white. They are communistic (bad) or democratic (good). People are Christians (good) or pagans (bad). We are either going to heaven (good) or to hell (bad). There is no in-between. This is where exclusiveness comes in.

If we can convince others that we are good and the rest of the world is bad, then they should, of course, want to be on the side of good. If we have the truth, then the bad guys must have falsehood and untruth. If God is on our side, then the others must be following the devil. So, naturally, it is our moral responsibility to show them their error, reveal to them our great truth, and get them to join the good. Thus they will be saved from evil. This either-or myth has influenced Christian teachings and attitudes from top to bottom, and has caused many bitter conflicts within Christendom. Each side in a controversy, convinced of having the truth, believes the enemy to be therefore in possession of falsehood and evil.

Fortunately, the world is not dualistic. It is not constructed of either-or situations or teachings or people. Dualistic thinking emerged in many cultures because the world is observably dualistic in some ways. There is some truth in an either-or world or the idea would not have survived so long and influenced so much. There is day and there is night . . . light and dark . . . war and peace . . . good and bad . . . black and white . . . sun and moon . . . male and female. It was natural for great systems of thought to be built upon the unshakable fact of these opposites.

Closer observation, however, discloses that dualisms are not so neatly opposite. When does night begin and day end? At 6 p.m.? At 8 p.m.? When the sun sets? When twilight ends? When the very last glimmer of light has completely and totally gone? Suppose it is night in Zürich, Switzerland, where I am writing at this moment. Is it also night in Lapland where the sun never sets? Is it night in a huge factory where artificial light keeps it just as light day and night? We cannot perfectly and precisely define night and day—it is an approximate truth or partial truth.

Men and women cannot be so neatly separated either. There is male and female in all of us. Some men deny their feminine qualities of intuition, tenderness, creativity, and try to be tough and "manly." Some women deny their masculine strengths, while others emphasize their masculinity by fighting for "women's lib." But according to the best insights of modern psychology, we are a balance, a mixture of male and female qualities with most of us having a preponderance of one sex or another. A few persons have an almost even balance of masculinity and femininity and endure great agony trying to decide which they are. So even in male and female, the great dualism myth is not absolute. It is a partial truth.

The either-or myth permeates much of the New Testament, as the Apostle Paul was trained in Greek dualism. And so we find him saying:

To set the mind on the flesh is death, but to set the mind on the Spirit is life and peace. Romans 8:6 (RSV)

... make no provision for the flesh, to gratify its desires. ... Romans 13:14 (RSV)

So, then, brethren, we are debtors, not to the flesh, to live according to the flesh—for if you live according to the flesh you will die, but if by the Spirit you put to death the deeds of the body you will live. Romans 8:12–13 (RSV)

With the division of the world into the saved and the unsaved, the enlightened ones and the savages, we find ourselves with the residue of that ancient inheritance, divided amongst ourselves, fighting over the most trivial nonsense.

Particularly unfortunate is the untruth that the body is evil and the spirit is good. The Greek philosophers taught this concept at least three centuries before Christ. In the Hebraic tradition, God made all things and called them good, breathed breath into them and gave them life.

So today, in the late twentieth century, we still think of our bodies as somehow unacceptable. We try to live in our heads as totally mental beings while both ignoring and abusing our bodies. This is a great tragedy for several reasons. Our thinking, cut off from the deep intuition and wisdom located in the body, has become sterile and unreal. We do not live and act as whole beings, the way we were created. And we are out of touch with the rich resources of the body for spiritual life.

Many modern movements, including some branches of psychiatry, help us to reunite our minds and bodies. Yoga, which is more and more widely practiced in the West, helps us to accept and attend to the wisdom of the body. The either-or myth has separated us from part of ourselves, an essential and enriching part.

As a consequence of the head-trip we are on, isolated from our "evil" bodies, we evaluate other religions on the basis of how they fit our *ideas,* not how they actually enlarge us when we experience them. How much easier for us, therefore, to categorize them as inadequate, pagan, or unchristian! To dismiss them at the head level is to deprive ourselves of the spiritual nourishment they contain.

If we are truly to find a religion for the whole man, a religion of full consciousness, we must learn to question all dualisms, all either-or thinking. When a friend asks us, "Was the lecture good or bad?", we can practice a response that rejects the either-or: "It was neither good nor bad; it was a great mixture of good, not so good, and not so bad. I have trouble thinking in either-or categories."

A religion of consciousness cannot divide the world into good and bad religions or persons or doctrines. It must seek the good in everything, reject what is altogether bad, and learn to live with that which is somewhere in between, transforming it into something more good when possible.

The Holy Man Myth

I have often witnessed the puzzling phenomenon of very intelligent men and women sitting at the feet of less intelligent, inexperienced religious leaders. These same persons will accept and believe the most ludicrous misrepresentations of reality from these leaders, primarily because they have been somehow set aside from ordinary humanity into a favored and special class known as the clergy. This is one symptom of what I call the holy man myth.

This myth may be summarized as follows: God has set aside a special group of people (mostly men, of course) who are not ordinary humans, but who have godlike qualities of moral perfection, freedom from temptation and sinfulness, and who are possessed with special wisdom. These men (and in a few rare instances, women) can answer all questions and solve all problems. They speak for God, know God intimately, and can make things right *for us* with God.

Very few people have dared to attack this myth. One mobilizes a wide front of opposition in speaking out against God's own chosen leaders. And those of us within the clergy, though well aware that the myth is a lie, still enjoy its special privileges enough that we don't want to spoil the show. Who wants to kill the goose that lays our golden eggs in the form of salaries, legal exceptions, and favored treatment?

I'm reminded of the friend who reaches for his glove compartment as he approaches the toll booth on the bridge, sticks a paper dickey complete with clerical collar onto his throat, pays a reduced rate, and speeds on as his free hand thrusts the now useless façade back into its resting place. I'm reminded of the friend who wears his clerical collar only when calling in the Catholic hospital, because there it brings him free refreshments in the coffee shop. I'm reminded of how I appreciate the income tax exemption for my housing allowance and a dozen other special loopholes for clergy that save me money each year.

The truth is that most of the clergy are not holy men or women at all. They are ordinary human beings who have studied a special set of books and passed their examinations while keeping their noses relatively clean. This means they cannot be flagrantly immoral, insane, or uncouth. While many of them have very sincere impulses to help others, and do so, that cannot be said for all.

The strange truth is that to become a clergyman, one does not need to be religious at all. One needs only to study what religion is all about. Most theological schools offer no training in how to pray or meditate. Many theological schools offer no training in working with or relating to persons. And so theological students come out steeped in ideas, but often unable to relate these ideas to actual life situations or persons. Theological schools are dominated by *scholars of religion,* few of whom are themselves deeply religious men or women. Many of these scholars have given no time to their own religious development. I make these statements from direct personal experience as a faculty member in several theological schools.

Within the clergy are some of the finest men and women I have ever met. But they are human. The best of them are well aware of their humanness, their sexual attractions, their selfish appetites, their angry and dark side. The dangerous ones are those who believe in the myth that they are somehow immune from human temptations and realities. They are the ones who end up running off with the choir director or becoming seriously depressed. Their dark side, lulled to sleep by their smugness about being "holy," erupts in some unguarded moment.

There are genuinely holy people in this world. They are also quite rare, and they may or may not be part of some official institution that sets them aside and calls them clergy. These holy men and women are well worth learning from, so long as we remember that they, too, have their human side, their limitations of wisdom and truth. We somehow want to find God in our midst, and so we try to elevate certain persons to a godlike status to satisfy the myth within us. It doesn't work. By setting up our own gods, be they clergy or not, we only ask for disillusionment.

The truth is that we cannot create religious leaders by educating them. Too many persons are drawn to religion as a profession for the wrong reasons: to escape the army, to feel clean themselves, to find a relatively easy life where one can talk his or her way to prominence, or to have an opportunity to exercise power. God often takes all these imperfect motives and uses them for his/her purposes anyway. I have often found God using my ignorance and my foolishness. I do not suggest that we should do away with religious leaders. That would be seeking self-mutilation. I am not attacking the clergy, but the *institution of the clergy* when its representatives are unfairly exalted and granted superhuman powers and privileges.

I ask only that we see our religious leaders for what they are: imperfect human beings who need us to challenge them and help them grow. Clergy are not complete, ideal human beings. They are often ignorant, often wrong, often inadequately educated. They need and require the input of their people in order to see reality whole. When we stand back and allow the clergy to make all our decisions for us, we are being cowards. When we allow them to make holy pronouncements about such subjects as marriage, sex, and abortion when they have never experienced any of them, we are foolish. We have bought the holy man myth.

It is time to recognize that at this moment the clergy are a deterrent to the growth of true religion in the world. They have an institution to protect and promote. They receive their brownie points by being good organization men and women. They get patted on the head when they defend the status quo in religion. Most of us within the clergy are not really free to be open to the currents of religious life and truth flowing around us. Our income, our futures, our retirement funds all depend on our defending the conservative institutions that support us. In spite of this, many clergy do a remarkable job of being honest and free. But it is important to be aware that religious institutions do not encourage openness, honesty, and truth in their leaders. Religious institutions, like many institutions, are more concerned with self-survival than with people or with truth.

I have often met lay persons far more enlightened and far more spiritual than the clergy whom they pay to serve them. These same lay persons feel helpless to bring change or growth to their congregations, because their holy man does not support it. The problem is that they allow one person to hold back the entire church, because they do not feel they can challenge the position of authority which the clergy claim. That claim is upheld by a laity still stuck with the holy man myth.

Closely related to the holy man myth, and one of its primary supports, is the dependency myth. I will try to show how these two are related.

The Dependency Myth

The clergy myth has flourished, as we have seen, because the Church has claimed special knowledge and special privilege for its leadership. Yet another reason is *within us,* in our dependency needs. Many of us, at some level of our consciousness, seek a parental figure on whom to depend. Feeling emotionally insecure, we are given reassurance by leaders who declare that they know the answers to life's deep questions. We make a contract with them. We agree to support the institution that they represent, and they agree to be authoritative for us.

Thus we may find successful lay men and women with very strong personalities but with an insecurity in spiritual matters turning to such leaders. I am convinced that when they go to church and encourage the holy man myth, they are governed by unconcious emotions, not by logic. When the lay person needs a strong authority figure, particularly if the person's parents did not provide that authority for him, the clergyman or woman becomes a substitute parent. And the lay person will of course be a "good child" who certainly does not contradict the parent.

This dependency is expressed in many ways. The government of the Church is left basically to the clergy, with some apologetic lay participation. Very often this amounts to rubber-stamping the decisions of the clergy. It is expressed more immediately in the structure of worship. The laity sit passively at the feet of the elevated clergy and listen. Spiritual growth of the laity is thereby severely stunted. They feel they have nothing to say in most churches, no insight to offer, no spiritual experience to inform the clergy or fellow members. They learn not to trust their religious experiences. This structure of worship keeps the laity children, sitting at the feet of their "adult" leaders.

The sad thing is that many of the silent lay persons have had deep religious experiences that could both enlighten and inspire their fellows. Put together, their religious experience far outweighs that of their one leader or staff of leaders. Yet they have no way to share that experience. They sit and listen, in spite of the overwhelming mass of data from communication theory about the crucial importance of dialogue.

Often the clergy really do not want dialogue, and I must assume from their behavior that most of them do not want their laity to become informed, alive, thinking, acting members. The passive dependency structure is too comfortable and the dependency needs of the people too strong to change a structure known to be outmoded and nearly dead.

There is a place for dependency. It is absolutely necessary under certain conditions. One is infancy. Infants cannot survive alone, and dependency upon their parental figures is not only appropriate but essential. In times of crisis such as emotional breakdown or serious accident, it is appropriate to turn to others and depend upon their help. Dependency is appropriate when we need information and someone has that information. Most educational structures are based on the assumption of that dependency need.

It is also important to know when dependency is inappropriate. As a child is growing up, the total dependency should be replaced by a relationship of equality as the child is ready to accept it. He grows out of dependency into equality as a fellow adult. But in the church we clergy do not wean our young. We tell them to keep coming back each week and begin with dependency again, sit at our feet yet another week, another year. It is a structure of permanent dependence, a religion for children in the faith. Is it any wonder millions are bored out of their skulls and will not come back?

To have an adult religion, a religion of full consciousness, for the whole man, we must give up this childish dependence upon our all-too-human leaders. In its place we need to learn how to trust our own insights, our own intuitions about God, our own legitimate religious experiences and leadings, whether they fit the Church's prescriptions or not. The dependency myth must go.

The Original Sin Myth

Over and over again, in my work with people in groups, I find individuals who do not believe in themselves. Take Dorothy, for example. Dorothy's parents did not know how to love her as a child. She did not experience enough early caring, and there was a gap in her nurture. As she grew up, the Church she knew reinforced her feelings of unworthiness. She was told repeatedly that she was sinful, depraved, and rotten to the core. Only God's great love and forgiveness could make up for this innate rottenness. Small wonder that at the age of thirty-four Dorothy was unable to love anyone, beginning with herself.

Two classical ways of viewing man are readily visible in our culture. One is to define him as innately evil, in need of divine intervention to be worth anything at all. This doctrine of original sin has been a strong thread in the Christian Church since very early days. A second approach is to reject original sin and assert the essential goodness of man. Man is capable of great creativity, beauty, and goodness, and was created "little lower than the angels." This humanistic view of man has been popular with poets and some philosophers, but has not been accepted by many religious groups.

It has taken modern psychology to help us see that both these views of man are naïve and harmful. Man is *both* good and bad. He is capable of both good and evil. If we stress his goodness and try to ignore what Jung calls the "shadow" side of man, that shadow side sneaks up on him and leaps out unexpectedly. We can see this in the behavior of "decent" people who suddenly betray a friend for their own purposes, of "Christian" nations bombing another nation into total destruction.

On the other hand, when we stress man's sinfulness and depravity, it becomes a self-fulfilling prophecy. Having no faith in her own possibilities for good, a Dorothy acts in ways that affirm her lack of self-worth and becomes a selfish bitch concerned only for herself. Look at one of the classical statements of this doctrine of original sin as expressed in the words of John Calvin, one of the leaders of the Protestant Reformation:

Every descendant, therefore, from the impure source, is born infected with the contagion of sin; and even before we behold the light of life, we are in the sight of God defiled and polluted. . . . From a putrefied root . . . have sprung putrid branches, which have transmitted their putrescence to remoter ramifications. . . .
Original sin, therefore, appears to be an hereditary pravity and corruption of our nature, diffused through all the parts of the soul, rendering us obnoxious to the Divine wrath, and producing in us those works which the Scripture calls "works of the flesh."[1]

This kind of thinking leads to defeatism. It can also lead to a total surrender to the Church as the one agency that can save us from our own evil selves. This is ultimately the purpose of the doctrine of original sin, of course. It binds us in lifelong dependence to the institution that claims to have the power to save us and deliver us faultless and pure to God. This doctrine is still actively taught by intelligent people today. The problem is that it reinforces the deep sense of unworthiness many people have anyway and leaves them in despair.

The truth is that we all have within us both light and darkness. The human potential movement in modern psychology is helping us to recognize that we need not settle for a limited life dependent upon the Church to give us a shred of self-appreciation. As human beings created by God, stamped with his/her image, we have immense potential for good, for growth,

1. *A Compend of the Institutes of the Christian Religion by John Calvin,* edited by Hugh Thompson Kerr, Jr. (Philadelphia: Presbyterian Board of Christian Education, 1939), p. 43.

and for the spiritual life. If we focus only on the dark side of our natures, we will not grow, because we will not believe we are capable of growth. If we focus only on the goodness within us, we are in danger of being overwhelmed by the darkness, the hate, the poison, the sin. But it is possible to look squarely at the darkness and acknowledge its reality and its power, and at the same time to see that there is immense potential for good within us. When we can be honest about both, we can move ahead in our pilgrimage.

The doctrine of original sin, claiming that we are born with an evil taint, is an abomination to mankind today. It is an ugly, monstrous doctrine that holds back man's evolution and development. It is a false teaching, not because it is untrue, but because it is only half true. Deep within the psyche of man, as plumbed by the pioneer psychologists, are beauty, goodness, a Self that seeks good as well as the darkness we can see as evil.

If we can recognize that potential for good *along with* the tendencies that hold us back, we can see new possibilities. The great spiritual leaders through the centuries have recognized this soul, this Atman, this Self which seeks release, and modern psychology is affirming the existence of this great force in man. I experience it as the presence of God within me, calling me into my full humanity. But naming it by that name is not essential. To recognize its presence, its power, its force for good, is essential.

As I read Jesus of Nazareth, he was realistic about the reality of evil, but *he believed in people.* He brought good news, but original sin is bad news, a myth we can no longer afford to drag along with us. Let's replace it with a realistic doctrine of man, a doctrine that recognizes the reality of both his good and his potential for evil. If we are to have a religion of full consciousness, we must do away with such half-truths as this doctrine of original sin and admit that within *our* consciousness is also the consciousness of God.

The Nice Guy Myth

One of the horrible misunderstandings of our faith that plagues us today is related to our understanding of love. We are taught that we should love our neighbor. So we go to church on Sunday and act "nice" to everyone we meet. We pretend to ignore the fact that some people irritate us immensely, that others make us angry by the way they manipulate us. We go on being "nice," smiling through gritted teeth—until we blow up at someone, or quietly organize a hate campaign against him, or pass on unverified gossip about his sexual life. This fact of Christian church life has led to the often justifiable charge that we are hypocrites.

The problem is that we have left the pain out of love. We have falsely identified loving each other with being "nice." But genuine love makes demands, one of which is the demand of honesty. If we love someone, we must not only tell him our positive feelings, but also level with him when he makes us angry and work through the response. This is often painful, and so we avoid the honesty. We find it equally difficult to share positive feelings. We may really care about someone, but we fear to tell him and so he goes through life never knowing of our positive regard until the day of his funeral. A little late.

Similarly, when we let our feelings of irritation and anger build up inside us, they find subtle ways to sneak out and do great damage. They come out in nasty little digs, in a tone of voice that cuts someone, in sarcasm and gossip. These are the "nice" ways to handle anger. It avoids the pain of direct confrontation, but must endure the deeper pain of wounded spirits and alienated friends who must continue to pretend they love one another.

The encounter movement has been teaching thousands of persons how to practice this deeper honesty, however. Such persons are increasingly uncomfortable in groups where they sense the phoniness of so many relationships.

Learning to express feelings directly to each other is more painful at first, whether in a church or in a marriage, but is infinitely more satisfying. It is painful to take a friend aside and say, "I wonder if you realize that I'm angry with you. Would you like to know why?" But the process of clearing the air can lead to genuine loving reconciliation. Making up is the best part of a good fight. To live by this style involves personal risk, possible misunderstanding, and the possibility of anger in return. To live by the alternative, the nice guy myth guarantees phoniness, a more vicious mode of handling conflict, and a feeling of uncleanness. To find a religion of full consciousness we must give up the nice guy myth and recognize both the love and the anger that are a part of our everyday relationships if we are human.

The Morality Myth

For millions of people religion means living by a strict code of conduct laid down by their church. They live by a list of should's and should not's, mostly should not's. This means their morality has an external source. It is located or centered outside the person in an institution to which they give allegiance.

This approach to morality has had positive influences in the emergence of civilized man. I do not doubt that. It has also had many negative side effects. For one thing, if I follow a strict code of behavior prescribed by someone else, then I must often reject my heart and its leading. The danger is that I become rigid and I turn off the messages from within myself that do not fit the moral code. This might mean that I am rescued from some horrible mistakes, for my "heart" might mislead me.

By following the code carefully, then, I avoid some mistakes, but I might also make some bad mistakes. I may also grow resentful, because the mistakes are not the mistakes I have chosen to make, but the mistakes the code has forced me into.

As an illustration, I would like to tell you about a man with whom I had a deep conversation on an airplane returning from French Canada. His wife had died ten years earlier, leaving him with a large family to raise. He shared with me why she died. His wife had contracted a deadly disease while pregnant. The doctors had faced the couple with the fact that the child must be aborted in the course of an operation which could save the mother's life. Their church refused to allow the operation, because it would certainly result in the death of the fetus. So both mother and unborn child died of the disease.

I asked my friend how he felt about having lost his wife that way. He said that he had been very bitter for a long time, but that he finally had come to accept it. He was a "good" churchman. He followed the moral code of his church rather than the dictates of his heart.

One of the incredible things I have learned from Jungian psychology is the moral strength of the unconscious Self within me. Jungians help you analyze your dreams and learn to trust your unconscious leadings by translating the dream language of symbols into plain sense. Amazingly, my inner Self is far more moral than my conscious self, despite the years of church attendance and theological studies my conscious self has undergone. But deep within me is the voice of God, speaking to me, leading me, guiding me if only I am willing to listen. When I hear that inner voice, I make far more moral decisions than when I ignore it. I feel cleaner, more whole, more together.

John A. Sanford speaks of this approach to morality:

Some psychologists of the Freudian school fail to see that there is a source of morality which originates neither from instinctual conscience nor from built-in morality of parents and society, but from

God in the sense of our own higher self, and which requires from us a morality which consists of following our own inner truth.[2]

It will be very difficult for us to learn to trust our inner morality more than our exterior codes. We certainly should not throw away the codes. We need them as a general guide, a checkpoint against which to evaluate the leadings of our inner voice. We need, as a society, to grow toward the trusting of the inner voice until we can eventually replace the rigid codes with a truer morality, God within. Perhaps for now we can resolve to treat ourselves and others with more charity when they have chosen not to follow the moral code of our society. Rather than automatically judging them, we might need to ask whether or not it is possible they are following a higher leading.

The obvious danger is that some persons will abuse their freedom if there is no universally enforced moral code to make them feel guilty and ashamed. Look at the world around you and you will discover they are abusing it. The existence of a universal moral code or universal Christian code is a myth. The choice is not to have a universal code or to have no code. The alternative is to begin trusting the personal moral voice deep within us which wants to lead us to behavior that will fulfill us and enlarge our spirits. This is a radical approach to morality, but I am certain it is one task of our emerging religion of consciousness to help us listen to that crystal inner voice. As Jung has said, "The unconscious mind of man sees correctly even when conscious reason is blind and impotent."[3]

2. *Dreams: God's Forgotten Language* (Philadelphia: J. B. Lippincott Co., 1968).
3. *Collected Works,* Vol. 11, edited by Herbert Read, Michael Fordham, and Gerhard Adler (New York: Pantheon Books, 1953), p. 386.

Some Other Myths

Many other myths should be helped to an early grave. Those mentioned above are particularly important to recognize, but the list could be much longer. One myth we drag along with us is the idea that God is masculine. We speak of God as he, his mercy and grace, his Son. It is extremely difficult to change deeply rooted language, but we should begin to recognize more consciously the equally strong and feminine side of God. God is neither masculine nor feminine, but the wholeness of both. To be fully conscious of God is not to know a him, but a presence.

The great sermon myth or preaching myth is another that is dying and should be buried. We have long labored under the mistaken idea that God speaks to people almost exclusively through preaching. (This is a particularly Protestant notion.) I have attacked this myth in an earlier book, *The Empty Pulpit.*[4]

Another myth that pervades our churches is the family myth. The really "nice people" are those who are together in family groups, who come to church every week and sit together as a family. In most churches the single person, the divorced person, the widow or widower, really is not fully accepted. We ignore such persons to our discredit.

The salvation myth is still another that needs review. This is the idea that some organization or group has the power to influence God on our behalf. They hold the keys for our salvation. As a result, if I please the leaders of that organization or group, I am virtually assured of a place in heaven. If I follow my heart in such a way that displeases those leaders, I may be

4. Harper & Row, 1967.

in danger of hell. This is an outgrowth of the either-or myth and the clergy myth. But it is certainly time to see it as nonsense. Only God holds God's keys.

I have been describing some of the furniture of the mind that I am convinced impedes our religious progress. And I cannot stress too often that the times are calling for a religion of the whole person who is both good and bad . . . sinful and divine . . . conscious and unconscious. To the extent we can begin burying some of our dead myths with appropriate appreciation for what they have contributed, we will be freer to live into the future.

Earth from outer space

4. GOD IN THE UNCONSCIOUS

begin this section with several very important assumptions. I believe in the existence of the unconscious. This is not a theoretical belief, as it was when I first studied it in college. I have been there. I have experienced my own unconscious in a variety of ways, particularly through examination of my dreams, meditations, and fantasies. The power of its contents to influence my life and the lives of those around me has been strongly documented.

My second assumption is perhaps more important. I reject the Freudian position that the unconscious holds only those contents repressed from our conscious life. I am totally convinced of the validity of the Jungian position, namely, that the unconscious also contains collective elements from all stages of life and history. Let me give an example from my own experience of this collective unconscious dimension within me.

At a time before I had experienced my first session of Jungian dream analysis, I had a vivid meditation in which I saw a beautiful eight-spoked wheel, glistening or glowing from within and rolling freely down a road. Later, I discovered that this wheel is a symbol from antiquity for the wholeness of the Self, related to the circle and the mandala, also symbols of wholeness.[1] It made even more sense when I discovered this reference much later in Neumann's monumental work on the history of consciousness:

1. I first discussed this symbol with Dr. Dieter Baumann, Jung's grandson, who helped me to see the rich, deeper meanings in the wheel symbol.

The "closed circuit" stage changes into one of creative balance, and, in place of the former static passivity, a dynamic constellation now assumes autarchic control. The appropriate symbol here is not the quiescent sphere, but the "self-rolling wheel."[2]

In my own conscious awareness I had no idea what a rolling wheel, making its own way down a road, could mean. But its meaning and content did not depend on my conscious experience. Rather, it drew meaning and reality from historical usage common to many cultures and peoples of whom I knew not. Dismiss this example if you will, but the accumulated data from thousands of similar cases defies easy dismissal. That wheel has become a dynamic symbol within me. I repeat my conviction that the unconscious is as Jung has claimed it to be, a dynamic source of incredible realities, some of which would subdue us and others that support, encourage, and inspire us toward wholeness and growth.

A third and terribly important assumption is also based on personal experience and supported by the empirical data of Jung and many others:

God is present in the unconscious. God comes to us, speaks to us, leads us and strengthens us through the unconscious if we are open to that presence.

I am not, at this point, interested in defining God. In the first place, I am convinced that it is not possible to define God. It does not bother me in the slightest that some persons would want to substitute another term for the one I use for deity, conditioned as I am by my Judaeo-Christian heritage. I do imply a reality, a center of that which is above, beyond, and yet within me, the creative principle of the universe, that which gives meaning and purpose to my life and to all life. It is that

2. Op. cit., pp. 301-2.

reality, that presence which exists in the unconscious of every man. The resources of that God are available to us in our unconscious. That is what I want to affirm with all my being. Beyond that, I prefer to describe some of the ways in which God appears in my unconscious, and may well appear, with infinite variety, in the unconscious of anyone, regardless of racial or national origin.

The Attainment of God

In 1952 a Roman Catholic scholar, Victor White, published a collection of essays (with a foreword by C. G. Jung) entitled *God and the Unconscious.*[3] White traces with some care the emergence of the concept of the unconscious in recent history, outlining the differences between Freud and Jung on this key concept and expressing many interesting opinions of his own.

White cites a fascinating book, never published in English, that appeared in 1848 written by Carl Gustav Carus, Court Physician to the King of Saxony. Carus referred to the unconscious as "the creative activity of the Divine." He stated that the task of the human mind is "to pursue the Divine within us in its unfolding out of the unconscious to consciousness." Again he said, "The highest aspiration of the conscious mind, the attainment of God, can be approached only by its submission to the deepest depths of what to us is purely unconscious."[4] We are only now really beginning to discover the amazing truth contained in these precocious words of a nineteenth-century physician. That God is found in the unconscious has only much later been elucidated by Jung out of his empirical studies of the actual data from the unconscious of his clients.

3. London: The Harvill Press.
4. Ibid., p. 31.

Here are a few instances from my own dreams of that activity in the unconscious which I attribute to God.

As a youth I graduated from college and spent a few weeks in the north woods of Wisconsin before taking up my new duties at Bradley University, where I had a faculty appointment. While there, I had a dream. Jesus appeared at my side in an ordinary business suit and clean-shaven. He asked a simple question: "Are you ready to come and help me?" In the dream I replied, "Yes, I think I am." That dream did not fit into my life context. I was delighted to be entering college administrative work, where I felt my career lay. However, the leading of the dream grew more intense in that next year, and I resigned my appointment and entered seminary, "just to try it out." Through an eruption from the unconscious in the form of a dream, I was led to follow God's intention for my life. While it was still I who made the choice, the leading was there in my unconscious. I have never regretted following that dream.

God's appearance in the unconscious may not be nearly so dramatic or obvious, however. A friend once told me that she had had a dream she did not understand. She was in Jungian analysis, and had been discussing her dreams with an analyst regularly for several years. The dream she did not understand was a situation where she was simply standing in a beautiful place. My interpretation of such a dream is that it is *a gift*. All beauty is of God, and is simply a gift from him, a reminder of his/her presence in us and around us.

I have occasionally dreamed of standing in a beautiful orchard, or of seeing magnificent beds of flowers, breathtaking in their beauty. One night not long ago I saw slowly emerging four petals of an intensely beautiful yellow flower whose center was of polished silver. The yellow of the petals glowed with the most intense color. Such an image is simply what it is, a vision of beauty, an expression of God's love and presence.[5] Similarly, in meditation, I often see images of breathtaking beauty which have no other purpose than to be. I feel warmed, lifted, honored.

A symbol I often see is a flowing spiral of color, whirling down into a dark center. On one occasion when this image appeared, I leaped down into the center of the vortex (using the practice of active imagination or active fantasy, which should be used only with guidance), and found myself falling into the pupil of God's eye. From there I found myself standing in God's stomach. Then I was standing in the hand of the deity, then flung up in the air as a father flings a child. In the next instant I saw a vivid image of a seven-sticked brass candelabra, slowly changing into glistening gold.

I had no idea why I should dream of a Jewish candelabra, and in doing some research on its meaning, I came to understand it as a historical symbol of God's light and presence. It is the symbol that stood beside the sacred ark, leading the Hebrews into the promised land. I have yet to live out all the implications of that candelabra's appearance in my psyche.

I know now, however, that the spiral is a sign of God. J. E. Cirlot reports that the spiral is a symbol of growth and evolution, an attribute of power, and an avenue by which man may "enter the beyond, through the 'hole' symbolized by the mystic Centre."[6] This is precisely what I had done in my meditation, long before reading this passage in Cirlot. I had entered the beyond and found it to be the eye of God.

Another common image is a series of eyes looking directly at me. These eyes are each different and unique. Some appear to be feminine in quality, others masculine. Some are the eyes of

5. I discussed this with Andrea Dykes, the analyst with whom I was working, and she agreed entirely with this interpretation.

6. *A Dictionary of Symbols,* trans. from the Spanish by Jack Sage (London: Routledge & Kegan Paul, 1971), pp. 305–6.

youth, others of more elderly persons. Some are blue, others dark. Some are very clear and distinct, others more blurred. Some are decidedly warm and friendly, others more detached. What do these eyes represent? What do they mean?

Not long ago a possible interpretation hit me, and it feels right. How does God see? The eye has historically been a symbol for God. Is it not possible that God "sees" us through our unconscious? Why should God not come in the form of many eyes—seeing and viewing us through the helping eyes of many?

I experience these eyes as interested, friendly, caring, concerned, and warm. This is also how I understand God in relationship to us humans. For me, it makes sense that God keeps his/her "eyes" on me, and that I can experience this relationship through my unconscious.

God in the Wind

Jung himself discusses an instance in which a god image appeared in the dreams of a young woman. She had come to him for analysis. In her dreams the young woman seemed to be making an inflated figure out of Jung, and he at first interpreted this to her as an example of the transference common to therapeutic relationships as well as to other authority relationships. Children, for example, often "fall in love" with their teachers. However, the tendency continued in her dreams, and seemed to Jung much too strong to be interpreted as an ordinary case of transference.

In the crucial dream that provided the key for Jung, a giant figure resembling her father stood with her on a hill covered with wheat fields. He held her in his arms like a child and the wind swept over the wheat fields. As Jung reflected on this, it occurred to him that she was in a real sense envisioning a *god* with superhuman attributes. The unconscious was trying to "create a god" out of the human person of the doctor-father, "as it were to free a vision of God from the veils of the personal."[7]

Jung also remembered that the wind is an ancient expression of God in several traditions. To the Hebrew, for example, the wind is the breath of God. It is God's spirit breathed into man to give him life. While the young woman was critical and agnostic where it came to a belief in God, her unconscious apparently had another bent. Rationally, she could not conceive of a deity. Nevertheless, as Jung says, "the dreams swelled the human person of the doctor to superhuman proportions, making him a gigantic primordial father who is at the same time the wind, and in whose protecting arms the dreamer rests like an infant." Jung adds that this "can only be described as a vision of God."[8]

John A. Sanford, an Episcopal priest who has studied at the Jung Institute in Zurich, has written a book entitled *Dreams: God's Forgotten Language.* Sanford documents his thesis that God has spoken to human beings through dreams throughout history. The Bible, he points out, is full of repeated instances in which God leads his/her people through the dreams of their leaders. Yet modern church scholars give almost no credence to dreams.

In one example Sanford describes a man who is dying from a critical physical illness. By working with his dreams, the man comes to the awareness that a terrible secret he fears to reveal is causing his illness. He finally decides to make a confession to the concerned persons rather than live in fear. In Sanford's words:

Tom's dreams led him into the only way he could follow to regain his health. They led like a thread from the labyrinth of his own thoughts to renewed healthy attitudes, to a free conscience, and to recon-

---

7. Jung, *Collected Works,* Vol. VII, p. 130.
8. Ibid., p. 132.

structed relationships. We may therefore assume an intelligence within his psyche, responsible for these meaningful dreams. For reasons which will appear more clearly as we go on, I do not hesitate to call this intelligence "God." God is the name men give to the purposeful, numinous power which crosses our lives; our dreams are one of the manifestations of this power.[9]

Antonio Moreno has discussed in depth Jung's views of the relation between God and the unconscious in his book *Jung, Gods, and Modern Man.* He discusses the theological problems he finds in Jung's thought, but affirms the basic point that Jung finds God as a dimension in the human unconscious. That God-image is a psychic reality in the unconscious, and Jung reports this as fact from his clinical work with patients over many years. Jung does not try to discuss the theological concept of God experienced as Creator or as transcendent, outside the human personality. He limits his observations to the data which he has observed in clinical work and does not speculate beyond that data. Moreno says, "The God of Jung is inside, and he calls a systematic blindness the prejudice that God is outside man."[10]

Other writers, including Charles B. Hanna, have discussed Jung's views on the relationship between God and the unconscious.[11] In the final analysis it is not Jung's views that are important, but how you as a person relate to that manifestation of God within you.

Jung asked himself:

Was the urge of the unconscious perhaps only apparently reaching out toward the person, but in a deeper sense toward a god? Could the longing for a god be a *passion* welling up from our darkest, instinctual nature, a passion unswayed by any outside influences, deeper and

9. P. 28.
10. University of Notre Dame Press, 1970, p. 83.
11. Hanna, *The Face of the Deep* (Philadelphia: Westminster Press, 1967).

stronger perhaps than the love for a human person? Or was it perhaps the highest and truest meaning of that inappropriate love we call transference . . . ?[12]

Jung tested his view with his patient, but she could not rationally accept it. A change began to occur, nevertheless, and she was soon ready to leave analysis.

So God appears in the unconscious. God appears in the form of many symbols: the wheel, the circle, symbols of other gods and goddesses, in shimmering images of beauty, in voices offering words of counsel, in symbols of light and fire, in convictions and intuitions. We are just beginning to learn the language of the unconscious, though the knowledge has been with us for thousands of years. Hidden within the language of the unconscious is a God-language if we are open to hear it.

A few additional symbols have historically been identified or associated with the deity. In Hindu, Persian, Greek, and Egyptian traditions, as well as in Islam, the sun is the eye of God (or Zeus, Allah, etc.).[13] The sun was worshiped in many cultures as the source of life and energy, and may be understood in some instances as a symbol of the activity of the divine.

Similarly, the eagle is often considered a symbol of deity, or as the messenger of the gods. Its ability to fly to great heights identifies it in primitive thought with the sun and light, an expression of divine majesty.[14]

Light is another symbol for God. Historically, God is associated with light before which man does not dare open his eyes. Moses' experience with the "burning" bush is an expression of this divine attribute. Jesus spoke meaningfully of light.

12. Op. cit., p. 130.
13. Cirlot, op, cit., pp. 317–20.
14. Ibid., pp. 91–93.

And Cirlot says, "Psychologically speaking, to become il-luminated is to become aware of a source of light, and, in consequence, of spiritual strength."[15] The rainbow is related to the light image and is yet another expression of God's presence and trustworthiness.

Many other symbols such as the fish, the trinity, and the quaternity have special religious significance to great numbers of persons. God appears in these unconscious symbols through our dreams, meditations, and fantasies, and so the unconscious may be seen as a source of the spiritual life, an avenue by which God reaches us.

But the unconscious is also frightening, and if we do not have firm ego boundaries, if we do not clearly know who we are, then our prior task is to develop that ego strength. Many people should not explore their unconscious because of the state of their emotional and mental stability. They must find God in other ways. But for those who are ready to explore out of strength, great riches and unlimited vistas await them.

15. Ibid., pp. 187–88.

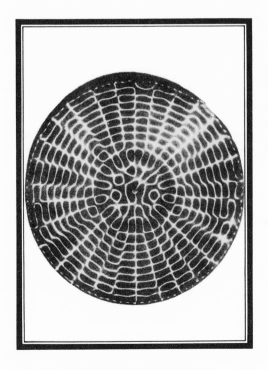

Sound wave vibrations

5. RELIGION OF
FULL CONSCIOUSNESS

About thirty young persons had gathered for the weekly chapel service at the Federal Youth Center. The chaplain introduced the story of Elijah with its image of the prophet hiding in a cave and experiencing wind, storm, and fire, then hearing the voice of God in the quiet stillness. He shared the 23rd Psalm with its image of the Lord as shepherd, and the 121st Psalm with its image of the hills and God as the source of help.

In place of a sermon or message, however, the chaplain did an unusual thing. He asked the worshipers to enter into a fantasy. He asked them to visualize themselves in a lush, green valley, an image provided by the 23rd Psalm. He asked them to see the blue sky and the clouds. On one side is a dark valley, on the other a wilderness with mountains beyond. He then asked them to cross the wilderness and climb into the mountains to a cave. He suggested that there might be something nagging at their minds, something they would like to ask for, or a question to which they wanted the answer.

When they reached the cave, he suggested that they might be weary and proposed that they lie down and sleep. When they awakened, the chaplain proposed that they now were in the presence of the Creator, and that they might ask the Creator the question that had been nagging them, or make a request. A period of silence followed.

When the chaplain interrupted again, he suggested that the Creator had a gift to offer each person before leaving the cave. "The gift might in some way be the answer to your question," he said. And again, quiet. As the meditation ended, there was strong feeling in the group, and some were in tears. Then came the invitation for anyone who wished to share his or her meditation with the whole group. Some did. Finally, the chaplain invited the worshipers to rise and move forward until all were standing hand in hand in a circle. The service was concluded. The deep impact of this approach to worship was attested by the comments coming to the chaplain for many days afterward.[1]

Religious approaches such as this are important for these reasons. First, the service tapped the deep resources of the imagination and the unconscious. And at least some of the participants found God there! Second, the minister allowed dialogue with and between the worshipers. They were allowed to talk and share, and the new man is one who insists on his right to dialogue. He is bored and impatient when he must sit passively and listen.[2] Third, the leader allowed for movement. The whole person was involved. The worshipers moved their bodies and made physical contact with each other. All three of these elements will be vitally important as we strive for a religion of full consciousness, and it is exciting to find that here and there, events such as this are happening.

If man is evolving into a new stage of his development in which there is greater communication between conscious ego and the contents of the unconscious, then is it not possible that we are ready for new religious styles that fit this new condition of man? This is a scary possibility, because it means leaving the old and familiar forms with the security they offer and launch-

1. Chaplain Mark Shedron of the Federal Youth Center in Denver, Colo., shared this experience with me and gave me permission to use it. Student chaplain Barbara Brewitt told me about the service and her personal response impressed me.
2. See my recent book, *21st Century Man Emerging* (Philadelphia: United Church Press [Pilgrim], 1971).

ing into the unknown. It is scary because the unconscious is scary. It is scary because God is scary. But along with the scariness is the excitement, the hope, and the joy of being a frontiersman!

The Old Religion

It is my conviction that our present religious styles are designed to address "Western man" with his tight lid on the unconscious and his preoccupation with conscious, rational thought. I shall make a few observations to this point, then go on to discuss the marks of this new religious style for man reclaiming his unconscious.

It seems only natural that as man moved away from his instinctive, primitive unconsciousness and developed his reason, his religion would become more rational. And so the sermon replaced the mysteries, and man thought *about* his religion. The more sophisticated religions became primarily concerned with beliefs and concepts, and the philosophically oriented theologians became the heros for awhile. Emotional expressions were considered uncouth, out of place. I remember sitting in church on a Sunday when the minister reminded the congregation that it was improper to call out "Amen" or "Hallelujah" during the service. A more primitive spontaneity was being squashed in favor of a more rational, middle-class, respectable style.

Today, however, there are many, many persons, myself included, who are hungry for more emotional expression in their religious life. We are, at the same time, unwilling to sacrifice reason and the intellect to find that emotional content. We want both, honoring the whole persons that we are. If you turn off my emotional side, I am left with dry, sterile intellectualism. If you turn off my reasoning power and want me to experience only feelings, then I am again half a person. I want my whole self involved in my religion, feelings and mind included.

It is possible, in line with this theory, that the mass in the Roman Catholic and Orthodox churches was basically geared to a more primitive level of man's development. I am not judging *primitive* to mean crude or bad or wrong." To the contrary, I am concerned to reclaim my own primitive self insofar as it will help me to live more fully now.

But the mass was a ritual drama that pointed to mysteries. One can feel the movement of the mass, hear it, smell it, sense the awe of being in the presence of something beyond without knowing the meanings of particular actions or words. As the Roman Church today tries to adapt the mass to Western man by translating the Latin mysteries into the local language and putting more emphasis on the sermon, there is surprising resistance. Perhaps many people wish to keep this connection with their unconscious represented by the more mysterious form of the mass.

On the other hand, the typical Protestant middle-class service tends to reinforce Western man, *talking about* his religious beliefs, verbalizing incessantly, and boring more and more people. As Victor White has put it, "If religion is found to be withering in Western man and society, is not this largely due to the fact that it has often become over-intellectualized, uprooted from its lowly origins in elemental, instinctive human needs and experience?"[3]

Religion in the twentieth century is a very complex phenomenon, and I do not presume to understand very much of it. I have simply offered a few thoughts that seem to me to fit with my general thesis that much current religious life is designed for a stage of man's existence we are ready to leave behind. This is not to suggest it is dead. Current religious approaches still feed

3. Op. cit., p. 45.

millions of persons. So long as people find nourishment in those practices, they should be offered. However, not all of us are in the same place, and *our interest in new forms must also be honored.*

If, indeed, man is becoming more and more open to the resources of his unconscious, and if God is present in the unconscious, then why not new religious styles that relate to the full range of human consciousness? I see such styles emerging in our midst, quietly and almost invisibly, reflecting the needs of the present for many people.

In the years immediately ahead we will see the new religious styles in at least two manifestations. First, will see them expressed in existing religious fellowships. Millions still find that church or synagogue membership is important to them; yet they are becoming new persons who want their religion to reflect their expanding consciousness. While many others cling to rituals and traditions of the past, some will be seeking a religion of full consciousness. The remainder of this chapter will discuss the ways I see this beginning to happen within existing churches.

Second, we will see the new religious styles outside the groups they have left behind and rejected. Many are turned off by traditional religious approaches. These persons will be discovering new depths within themselves and getting in touch with their spiritual selves. The closing chapter will be directed to them.

Church Styles for the Future

I want to suggest five dimensions of the new religion of consciousness as it may affect the life of a traditional church. The first dimension is that of increased awareness of self, others, and environment.

A primary cause of boredom with traditional church experiences is the lifeless repetition of rituals whereby individuals are nothing but bodies filling seats, staring at the backs of each other's heads. There is need for personal contact, interaction with each other.

On a bright November morning I arrived at a Thanksgiving chapel service at the theological school where I was then teaching. There was a printed order of service. We began by singing hymns. I felt a bit uneasy. I had some good news to share with those friends, and the printed order of service did not encourage me to believe I would have the opportunity. My wife had just given birth the evening before to a healthy baby boy. I had been present at the delivery, and was still moved by the miracle of human birth. I therefore wanted to share the good news and that miracle with my friends in the chapel.

I continued to feel frustrated. A period of silence was observed in which we had time to reflect on our inner feelings of thankfulness. Then, in place of a message, we were invited to share our feelings with the whole group, and there was general delight, joy, and applause as the assembled congregation entered into my good news. My misgivings, conditioned by years of being treated anonymously in churches, were misplaced that glad November morning. I left feeling great.

Why was that service so special? I am convinced it was a prototype of one direction churches must move if they are to remain alive in the coming age. The service allowed me time to relax, breathe, and feel into my own depths. The silence let me get in touch with the sense of relief and joy that was in me that day. It gave me the opportunity for increasing my self-awareness, though I could have sat rigidly out of touch just as easily. The choice was mine, and I had the opportunity if I chose to use it. It is equally possible to sit through a sermon, never hearing a word, daydreaming or sleeping.

The service also allowed me to share my feelings. It allowed private worship to become corporate worship as the entire room shared my happiness. The feelings expressed from the pews that morning became the heart of our celebration. Worship had moved from the people toward God, rather than from the minister's study toward the pews—the generally sterile pattern of worship. It was two-way communication. It was dialogue. The worship belonged to us, not just to the leader. And it was a time of joy.

There are now many tools that can help deepen the life of a group. Most persons in a religious congregation do not know each other, do not trust each other, and often do not like each other. Not long ago I spent a day with thirty persons, mostly from one congregation in Granite City, Illinois. We met in a large carpeted room under a domed roof designed by Buckminster Fuller. It was an impressive setting. And we did some very simple things. We stretched and breathed deeply, getting in touch with the fact of our bodies and celebrating our physical selves as good. We shared the tears of a young woman whose mother had died a few weeks before. We sat in twos and shared some of our feelings with another individual.

At one point each person chose a single flower from a pile in the middle of the room and spent some time in silence, studying the flower, meditating on it, letting it move the imagination—and then sharing some of the thoughts and feelings that emerged. At lunchtime it was noted that only some had brought a sack lunch; the others obviously had not gotten the message to do so. Instead of sending the lunchless ones out to find the cafeteria, we enacted the feeding of the thirty. We put all the food we had on a large table, cutting the sandwiches into smaller units, and invited everyone to eat. Lo and behold, there was enough to eat and some left over! We touched and talked and accepted ourselves as okay human beings. We celebrated a beautiful, simple day together.

The result was trust, growing and flowering in that group. The very simple experience of relaxing into our humanity allowed a congregation to deepen its life to some extent. People shared their feelings, touched each other's person, and listened to their own inner depths for a time. A religious congregation thus became a human fellowship rather than an assemblage of strangers.

Encounter in the Church

A second dimension of the new religion of consciousness that can enrich the local church is encounter. Encounter groups are deep, intensive groups led by highly skilled and trained persons. In such groups people talk about their deep, personal problems and concerns. They try to understand and change the behavior patterns that block them from full human functioning. They cry out their grief, scream out their rage, and allow their tenderness. When there is enough trust in the group, love is released and a powerful climate for growth evolves.

Many persons agonize over self-revelation, fearing rejection by others. "If they really knew my secret, how rotten or inadequate I am, they would throw me out." Amazingly enough, the reverse happens. For when we share our pain with others, they can identify with us at a deep, loving level, rather than superficially. They know they hurt; they will know we hurt also, making intensive community possible.

Encounter is a much deeper level of relationship than the awareness level I have described. It touches the unconscious much more deeply and openly. Many people are not ready for this experience, a fact that must be honored. Many people, as we have seen, are too frightened of touching their unconscious. It may be too painful. It may be too fragile. They may have only a tenuous hold on their egos, and opening their door to the unconscious may be too much of a strain. In such instances it is well not to insist that they experience encounter. It can be shattering to them. The majority, however, given some ego strength to work with initially, have come out of such intensive groups stronger and more self-accepting. The evaluations I have received from countless groups very strongly indicate this growth factor.

Some research has indicated that encounter has questionable value. Some of the research has questionable value as well. One revelation of the research is the importance of the group leader. A hostile leader, an unskilled leader, or a voyeuristic leader can do harm instead of good. Jerry and Elisabeth Jud have done an important piece of research on persons who have attended their "Shalom retreats," a deep encounter experience designed for personal growth.

Through careful follow-up studies, gathering data from the participants and others close to them, reinforced by the use of psychological tests, the Juds found significant growth in over 90 percent of those who attended. I have personally seen significant life changes in many, many persons who have come to a deeper acceptance of themselves through encounter experiences. I have seen them over a period of months and years following the encounter experience. Those changes were not imagined.

Religious experiences are also to be found in genuine encounter, where people meet each other at a deep emotional level. When the National Training Laboratories began their human relations workshops in the late 1940s, one of the persistent reports from participants was that their T-group experience was the most religious experience they could remember. That was a bit perplexing to the social scientists who invented the T-group, but people continued to speak of the experience as a religious one. Many clergy were drawn to those laboratories as a result.

The phenomenon is not a great mystery to me. The human

being in his depths is a spiritual being. When I look deeply into myself, I find God waiting there. I find religious dimensions in me that I had not suspected. I am religious—related to the cosmos, to all life, to all living creatures. So it is not surprising to me that when two persons meet at a deep level, whether through soul-sharing conversation, the sharing of joy and pain, or through sexual and personal intercourse, it is a spiritual experience. That is why encounter experiences have a religious dimension when led by a loving and trusted leader. That is why encounter experiences have deep values to hold out for the enrichment of existing religious groups.

Psychologist William Schutz, a key figure in the encounter movement, writes knowingly:

> The encounter group offers a method for feeling and exploring many religious abstractions. When encounter focuses on the inner self, mystical experiences begin to occur. Combining the encounter group with the religious experience has helped me to elevate my aspirations for the encounter group. To look for the God in you, and to get in touch with your cosmic energy, have become meaningful pursuits and seem to redefine what I earlier took as encounter goals.[4]

Here again we see the world becoming the bearer of man's religious life. The churches can open themselves to the use of encounter, or stand by as the world becomes religious outside the churches. Encounter has much to offer the churches. I have worked as a consultant to one church since 1971, offering an intensive growth-encounter weekend twice a year for members of the group. By their own claims, some significant changes have come in individuals and in their modes of relating to one another.

4. *Elements of Encounter* (Big Sur: Joy Press, 1973), p. 96.

The Contribution of the East

A religion of consciousness also needs the insights of Eastern *3)* religion, and this is the third dimension on my list. Religions of the East have always stayed in closer touch with the human unconscious than have the more rational, conscious religions of the West. These religions have remained more conversant with the imagination, the intuition, the mystery of man's extrasensory faculties, and the inner world of fantasy. If we in the West are to find religion of full consciousness, we can learn a great deal from the Eastern approaches. Both conscious, rational mind and unconscious, mysterious depths are critically important. But a judicious blending of both can bring us a more balanced, more whole, and more exciting religious life.

The blending of the East with Western religion has long been in process, and we can see its effects in many places. The chaplain's use of a fantasy experience to lead his worshipers into a sense of God's presence is an example of Eastern influence.

The practice of meditation is growing throughout the West, yet it is rarely found within the churches. For the most part, individuals are discovering meditation by joining a yoga class, a T-M (Transcendental Meditation) group, or some other group like Arica, in which meditation is taught and practiced. I do know of some churches which offer yoga and meditation classes, and of some church leaders who are using meditation as a part of their program or as an element in their services of worship.

Meditation can be employed to help the meditator escape the world of the senses and live in a world of fantasy, and Westerners have long rejected it as escapism. To be sure, some people use meditation as a way of escaping the world of responsibility and pain. Communion wine can also be misused.

On the positive side, meditation can open to us a world of mystery, beauty, and inner peace. Through meditation we can listen to the leading of our unconscious. We can find God's leading there. No one can be convinced of the value of meditation by reading about it or by studying it in books. That is a head trip. Only by trying it, practicing it, and studying the effects in our lives can we discover whether or not meditation is for us.

Other Eastern influences are also very important for Western religion to help us reclaim the wholeness we need so urgently. Yoga is a body discipline that has deep spiritual implications entirely apart from the Hindu tradition out of which it has come. Yoga is a simple, quiet method of stretching and relaxing the body so it is more vibrant, more together, more flowing. Since I have learned yoga, I am more in touch with what is going on in my body. I tend to listen to my stomach when it says, "Stop! I'm full. That's enough." Before, I would keep eating because it tasted good. I was eating for my mouth, not for my bodily needs.

When I am doing my yoga postures with some regularity, I feel more alive. I am more in touch with my breathing and with the life within me. Meditation is more alive because the flow of messages within me is freer. I believe it is a deeply religious matter whether or not I am relating positively and deeply with my body.

The East also offers a variety of meditation styles that involve the movement of the body, such as the very ancient Tai Chi Chuan, or Chinese walking meditation. Laura Huxley has spoken of it in these words:

As Tai Chi Chuan becomes part of Western culture it will probably develop in many different ways, as it will have a different meaning for each individual or group. Generally, however, it produces a union of inner and outer, of body and soul, of contemplation and action—all of this on the nonverbal level.[5]

Gia-fu Feng, Chinese sage and author, has written of it:

Tai Chi Chuan is a form of meditation in movement. It is a way of centering, aiming at sensomotoric awareness and body alignment. It corrects the posture and enhances relaxation. It energizes the body and tranquilizes the spirit. It is a bridge between Eastern meditation and Western psychotherapy, integrating the mind and the senses.[6]

Western religion has overemphasized the conscious and the verbal and rejected the body. But many of us are now ready for religious practices that help us bring mind and body together again.

Sadly, for the many people who are hung up on the either-or myth—something is either Christian or it is of the devil— Eastern religion cannot offer its richness. It is dismissed with contempt or revulsion because it is not "Christian." If we believe in one God, we can hardly dismiss two-thirds of his/her world as having nothing to say to us. God's presence is everywhere and we can find God and learn from him/her in a million forms.

Dream-sharing Groups

The importance of taking dreams seriously is the fourth dimension on my list. If it is true that God appears in the unconscious, and if our dreams are one important avenue to the unconscious, then the study of dreams and their meanings in our lives should be a very natural step. I don't know of many places where people gather to study their dreams, but I am

5. Gia-fu Feng and Jerome Kirk, *Tai Chi—A Way of Centering and I Ching* (New York: Collier Books, 1970), p. 3.
6. Ibid., p. 3.

planning to experiment with groups in which we will help others to evaluate the meanings of dreams as a key to personal growth.

In an encounter group I led recently, there was a dramatic illustration of the importance of a dream for one member. The group gathered for the first time on a Friday evening, and we spent some time in getting to know one another. Next morning one young woman in the group reported that she had had a strange dream and didn't understand it. In fact it frightened her. In the dream the group had been gathered around one of the members, whom I shall call John. John was dying, and was covered with a sheet, according to the young woman, Barbara (also a pseudonym). "Why should I dream such a morbid thing?" she asked. "I hardly even know John."

I asked Barbara if she had felt morbid about the funeral during the dream. She replied that she hadn't. In the dream it hadn't been a sad occasion at all. In fact she had felt rather good about the funeral in the dream. I suggested that perhaps there was some dimension within her that was ready to be buried, and that possibly John symbolized that part of her. She protested, "But I hardly know John. How could he represent some part of me?" I had no idea, but asked her to reflect on it as we continued.

In the course of the weekend John disclosed to the group that he often felt like a misfit, and that he wanted to do something about it. As a result of John's work on his feeling of being a misfit, Barbara had a revelation. "That's it!" she said. "That's the part of John that is also a part of me! I had no idea John felt like a misfit until he said so. But *I have been* too to some extent. My parents wanted a boy, so I have tried to be the son my father didn't have. I was a tomboy, and that part of me is what I want to give up now."

That was a joyous discovery for her, so the entire group

gathered around an imaginary "grave" constructed with pillows covered by a blanket, and we had a funeral for the "misfit" part of Barbara. We helped her bury it. We sang and danced and celebrated with her the death of her "misfit" self, and we affirmed her femininity.

In discussing other persons' dreams as a group, I was pleased to see that the principle of group riches held true. One member of the group could see the place of one symbol in the dream, while another extended the meaning of something else. By sharing our insights we made remarkably good sense of some rather strange dreams. As a result of these experiences I see a big future for dream-sharing groups. Training and expertise will be required, as with any other group. If leaders are not trained in the study of their own dreams, the groups will be limited in their ability to help people, and should not attempt to do so. But with trained leaders, the possibilities for bringing conscious and unconscious into cooperative unity are unlimited.

More Creative Worship

Innovative, creative worship is the fifth dimension of this new religion of consciousness that can bring life to our churches. I have just come from a "creative worship service" offered by a well-meaning church. I have come away depressed. To be fair, there were some "creative" elements in the service. We introduced ourselves to persons sitting near us. We sang two folk songs accompanied by guitar and tambourines. We heard a recorded song from a hit musical. The mood of the service was fairly relaxed and informal. And following the minister's meditation, he allowed a few minutes for questions from the congregation, looking at his watch regularly as he answered.

At the same time, the service had the same stifling clergy-heaviness that turns so many people off in traditional Protestant services. The order was decided in advance and printed. While informal, the minister spoke through most of the service. His voice dominates my memory of the morning. There was no chance to express or share the concerns with which I went to the service, no chance to offer *my* prayers, express *my* anguish, receive ministry from my fellow worshipers. The whole service was built around a concept the minister wanted to communicate, ignoring *our* needs to communicate. I have come away knowing that a few minutes spent in quiet meditation in my living room would have fed my spirit far more than the clergy-centered bombardment I had suffered. While I am a man who hungers for meaningful worship, I will not go back.

Let me describe a contrasting experience. I arrived for an evening session of my creative worship class one evening not long ago. A subgroup within the class had planned a service for that evening. We were invited to go quietly into the adjoining room, which was in darkness except for a few candles lit at the far end. Each of us found a small candle in our chair. As we stood quietly in a circle, we were invited to "dump" any of the garbage we had brought with us into an empty container in the middle of the room.

We stood awhile in silence, getting in touch with the "garbage" we might want to be rid of, then listened to some readings from the Scriptures on the theme of light. I told of a dream I once had had in which Jesus handed me a lighted candle. I started on my way, shielding the candle to keep it lit. But then my own breath blew out the candle. I returned to Jesus who stood by a candelabra, the symbol of God's presence. I told him I had blown out my own candle. He did not judge or blame. He simply relit my candle and handed it back to me. Again I blew out my own light. Again he lit it silently.

In that darkened room I stood with the group and reflected on the power of my dream and its present meaning in my life.

We heard the words being read: "You are the light of the world. Let your light so shine. . . ." And a flame was passed from person to person until all our candles were lit.

Before we left the room, we sat in the semidark and shared some of our concerns. One member of the group faced a major operation in the near future, and he told us the implications. Another had just felt the life of his first child move in his wife's belly, and he was alive with the celebration of that great discovery. And so we shared our lives with one another, and it was a sacrament.

That was worship for me because I was deeply involved, yet I was related to some ancient traditions as well. I could share what was deeply on my heart, and it was heard and responded to. The service was informal and open to spontaneous events.

Churches which are seeking the religion of full consciousness will need to offer both creative worship that arises from the hearts of the people as well as more traditional forms for those who want them continued.[7] There is no reason why worship should not involve the full being of persons—the mind, the senses, the movement of the body, the riches of the unconscious. As it is today, we are offering worship that is impoverished, worship that arises from the clergy, not from the hearts of the people.

Future church leaders will need to learn how to be more comfortable with unconscious phenomena, rather than avoiding it or dismissing it as so many do. If the churches are to move into the future, its leaders will need to study not only the importance of dreams, biofeedback, fantasy and meditation, but how to be comfortable with the experience of their own unconscious. It cannot be merely academic study, in other words.

7. See my book on creative worship, written with Jerry Kerns, *Let It Happen: Creative Worship for the Emerging Church* (New York: Harper & Row, 1973).

Admittedly, this means seeking professional guidance to look more deeply into ourselves, then to lead our people in their exploration of the unconscious.

We can only guess at the many additional ways in which this evolutionary development must influence future church life. We must be willing to use our imaginations and be open to exciting new changes, or the churches will die with the old man, living in his head, and the imaginative future of religious man will be lived out outside the walls of the church.

A geometric yantra used in meditation

6. SPIRITUAL
BUT UNCHURCHED

Many people who have turned away from organized religion nevertheless feel themselves to be spiritual. They have had some mystical experience or have felt the deep transcendent dimension in themselves, yet they are not comfortable in a structured religious ritual. They know there is some truth in religious realities, but they do not want to belong to a church or a synagogue.

And why should all people be expected to express their religious sentiments and concerns in the same way? It is this unchurched group of people who are yet returning to some depth of faith whom I wish to address in this chapter.

There are at least four basic styles open to the person who does not belong to an organized religious denomination. One is to have no religious life at all. While many people choose this path, it is very difficult to eliminate all religious phenomena, because spiritual realities are present in the unconscious of every living person.

A second style is to find a guru or master and sit at his feet, symbolically or actually. There are many today who set themselves up as gurus and enjoy disciples coming to them to learn and, in effect, worship them. Some of these gurus are from India or other cultures where the guru-disciple syndrome is more common, and by their uniqueness of speech and dress they attract adoring crowds. The most current guru figure is the teen-aged Maharaj Ji, who has drawn enormous crowds and has many devoted followers.

I once spent a few days at a yoga camp in the Canadian mountains where a well-known guru from India led yoga sessions in the summer. A few days were enough for me. We were awakened by a bell at 5:30 a.m. At 6 we were seated in the meditation hall, and the doors were locked so latecomers could not get in. The master then read the list of nearly two hundred names, publicly chastising those who had missed meditation the day before and assigning to them as punishment such jobs as carrying out the garbage or washing dishes. (Love is not having to say you're sorry?)

We chanted and meditated for several hours, then moved outdoors for an hour of hatha yoga in the sunlight. I noticed that the guru barked orders like a drill sergeant but did not do the postures with us. There were only two meals a day, and it was announced that we were being put on half-rations due to the unexpected expenses of a special project of the guru. I wish to assure my readers that full rations were nothing to get excited about, and half-rations with the first meal of the day served at noon left something to be desired.

For one meal, I happened to be seated at the elbow of the master himself, and I thought it would be a good opportunity to ask him a few questions and learn something of his life. I even had the audacity to feel that I might have an idea or two that would be interesting or helpful to the great man. But, alas, he brought a magazine with him, and proceeded to read throughout the meal, totally ignoring those of us at his table. He never spoke once nor acknowledged the existence of those around him. I was also amazed when waiters brought special helpings of steaming food to the guru not served to the rest of us. That helped to explain why the master was becoming paunchy. And he was one of the most highly publicized gurus in North America! It didn't take long to decide that that man could not be *my* master. In order to follow a master, one must close one's

eyes to many of the person's shortcomings. In effect, we are looking for a god, an infallible being with all the answers, a security blanket. We will not find that in a human.

I decided that gurus should be sized up with the same care I take in sizing up any leader. When self-proclaimed religious leaders demonstrate more interest in their own publicity than concern for human beings, I lose interest.

I remember the famous American preacher whose books I had appreciated. On one occasion I visited his church with a friend who worked on his staff. At the coffee hour following the service, my friend took me up to meet the great person. As I opened my mouth to say something, I felt a strong tug on my arm. I was pulled grandly past as his eyes had already gone on to the next person waiting to speak to him. There was not only no human contact, but it was a degrading and dehumanizing experience.

Gurus should be tested by their deeds as well as by their words, just as any teacher, minister, or leader should. If the guru owns luxurious homes and rides in fancy automobiles, it somehow negates the spiritual message he claims to be bringing to the world.

In spite of these warnings, many people will find the guru path a viable option for them. It is one way to express one's religious longings, study religious teachings, and attempt to improve one's life.

A third alternative to being churched but religious is to join a semireligious group that has goals and ritual practices that fit one's individual goals and feelings. For many youth today, joining a commune or extended family serves this function. And not only youth. It is a natural instinct to want to belong to a group that will accept and support you. When a person cannot feel that existing churches can fill this need for them, for whatever reason, communes are one alternative.

Another form that this third option takes is the underground church or house-church group, which is organized independently outside existing churches, yet which continues some traditions of those churches.

As I have observed such groups, and my experience has been severely limited, one of the primary obstacles to success as a commune or extended family is the handling of hostility. (This same problem prevents depth in most churches, incidentally.) Just as in many families, group members often have difficulty handling conflict creatively. When leadership is not clearly defined; when anger builds in individuals because roles are not clarified, trouble is inevitable. When there is no open expression of the unavoidable anger that develops in a family, it becomes like a cancer that eats away from inside. When honesty and openness prevail in such groups, they can be an exciting option for the spiritual hunger and dependency needs of today's non-church person.

There is a fourth alternative or style. And that is to be your own man—or woman. It is possible to be a spiritual person who does not belong to a church, nor to a group, nor who sits at the feet of a master. It is difficult but it is possible. I do not recommend it, nor do I recommend any of these four styles of life. The path which is right for you is the one that fits best and meets your needs most fully. It may be that you feel the need of a close, supportive group at this time. You may have different needs at another time, particularly if you continue to grow.

It is possible to be your own person. You can be your own person and learn important truths from some of the gurus without buying their total package of doctrine and devotion to them. It is possible to learn spiritual disciplines from a group such as Arica without following the same master. It is possible to learn great and vitally important truths through working with a Jungian analyst without becoming a Jungian. In the final

analysis, we are individuals, though nourished and strengthened by groups, teachers, families, and leaders of many kinds. When we die, we leave them all behind anyway and face our Maker alone.

Another form of this style is to find a group or teacher that encourages individual growth from dependence to interdependence, from childhood to maturity. The tragedy with so many churches, groups, and gurus is that they foster childlike dependence on them rather than helping the individual to grow. As a teacher and counselor myself, I see my goal as helping people to grow past the point of needing my support. Each of us has within himself the strength and resources to be his own person, depending upon no master. Sadly, most of us have not been taught to believe in our own potential to grow, to expand, to find that deep inner strength. Too many hucksters surround us who want us to need them. But a religion of full consciousness will ultimately help the individual stand alone, finding strength and support here and there when it is appropriate, but living maturely without that support when it is unnecessary.

In order to reach this lofty goal, you must be desirous of growing more than leaning. You must expose yourself to feedback and pain in order to know yourself fully and deeply. And you must be willing to fall back for support when you need it, move out again when your strength has returned.

The truth is that we do not need to depend on any church or religious group to tell us that we are okay. We do not need to satisfy any ritualistic formulas laid down by a hierarchy of fellow humans in order to be acceptable in the sight of God. That okayness is only between us and God. It is not a human right to tell us we are or are not acceptable to God.

It is also true that you are a spiritual person whether you are comfortable in a religious group or not. You have deep spiritual resources within you. You have God within you, and no one can take that away. You can be your own person and stand in your own dignity as a spiritual being.

Whether any of these options appeal to you as an individual, I believe the new religion of consciousness has begun to emerge. Some of the marks of this new religion of full consciousness are worth noting.

More Spontaneous Religion

One of the marks is that religion is becoming less routinized and more spontaneous. Religious experience, we are rediscovering, cannot be legislated for a particular hour of every week. One may discover religious experience in a forest walk on Thursday afternoon, in deep conversation with a neighbor on Friday evening, in a Tuesday morning yoga class, or in a silent moment on one's knees.

Just as the unconscious itself cannot be predicted, and just as God's activity is dynamic and spontaneous in the moment, so a religion that includes these factors cannot be totally predictable and comfortable. We cannot keep God in little boxes, letting him/her out for an hour on Sunday mornings for a nice chat! God simply won't stay put.

People are also realizing that religion is not something one joins; it is something one is. You are a religious being because you are alive. Our relationship with the divine is within us; no organization has the power to let us into that relationship or rule us out. We more and more reject the presumptuous claim of any organization to legislate our relationship to God. No group can rule us out of heaven or out of the human race because we have broken its regulations or rejected its doctrines. To claim that tyrannical power is the gravest blasphemy. That is a matter of relationship between God and the individual. Religion is not a matter of power politics, but of the inner soul.

(The *implications* of one's religious experience may and should be reflected in one's social behavior and political action.)

So the new religious style will see less emphasis on huge organizations that require allegiance to maintain huge budgets and buildings. There will be more relaxed acceptance of religious experience in temporary structures and momentary experiences—in a dream, a meditation, an inspiration, a chance gathering, a moment of crisis. (I am remembering what a powerful religious experience it was for some of us facing crises and danger together in the racial struggles in America in the 1960s, for example.)

There is a strong cultural current to swim against when individuals adopt this attitude toward religion. For many millions of us there is a sense of guilt if we are not in church on Sunday morning or in synagogue on the sabbath. We are victims of a mentality that is more interested in maintaining institutions than in meeting our genuine religious needs. I believe church services are fine for those who still find them meeting their spiritual needs and interests. But the assumption that those of us who do not find our needs met in the same way are somehow unwholesome, unacceptable, or "unchristian"—that attitude is really juvenile. If we buy the guilt some "religious" leaders would lay on us because we do not support *their needs* to have a full house on Sundays, that guilt can blind us to genuine religious events in our lives.

One sign of the new approach to religious styles is the emergence here and there of study-meditation centers, which combine classes on human growth and psychology with religious practices such as meditation drawn from many traditions.

Many people will continue to find the great traditions of organized religion meaningful and powerful. The history they represent can be experienced as a living stream of vitality and power. I know such rituals occasionally lift me and feed me. But to expect the same people to come in and find that meaning in the same way week after week and year after year is unrealistic. It is like eating the same meal day after day after day. That only dulls our appetites.

Openness to All Religions

A second mark of the new religious attitude is an openness to truth and light from all traditions. All religious expressions, from the most primitive to the most sophisticated, have some validity and something to teach us. There is a new spirit of openness to learn from the ancient disciplines, and this is an exciting fact of our age. In every corner of the United States one can find yoga classes, Zen meditation groups, Sufi study groups, people reading the Tibetan Book of the Dead or consulting the ancient Chinese book of wisdom, the I Ching. Where we once laughed or dismissed ancient doctrines carelessly, we now find spiritual depth, intuitive wisdom that feeds and informs us today.

The religion of the American Indian is an interesting illustration. Once disregarded as savage rituals, the age-old dances and songs are now understood as the religious myths of a noble people. In a book such as Frank Waters' *Masked Gods,* on Navaho and Pueblo ceremonialism, we find deep appreciation for the spiritual depth in Indian mythology.[1] Waters draws the fascinating parallels between some American Indian concepts and those of Buddhism and even of modern depth psychology! The intuitive wisdom of the past has incredible riches to offer if we allow it to speak to our deeper selves.

It is precisely at the level of the unconscious that persons are united with all humanity. As we dream or meditate, we discover

1. New York: Ballantine Books, 1950.

symbols in our unconscious that flood in from every stage of human existence and prior to human existence. Jungians call this the collective unconscious, one of the most fascinating phenomena now under conscious scrutiny. So a religion of full consciousness should begin with the realization of the deep, underlying unity of all human beings.

No one religious approach has all the answers. No church has a corner on truth, despite the urgency of a church's presumptuous claims. No one creed, no one answer, no one approach is complete, perfect, all-satisfying. The realization of this incompleteness, of God's continuing, unfolding revelation in this very moment, is a hallmark of the new religious attitude. It leads to reverence for the now, for new truth that may be revealed to you or me today! It also leads to a little more balanced view of those who claim the final truth was delivered to them. There is one world and one people. There is but one God whose truth and presence comes in many forms. We cannot afford to sneer or to turn our backs on any path.[2]

The Human Potential

A third mark of the new religious style is a basic acceptance of human beings as creatures of worth. Many of us have been raised on religious teachings which so stressed how rotten man is that we have had difficulty believing in ourselves. An equally naïve position is to assume that man is totally good. This neglects the reality of the dangerous shadow side in each of us.

But there is a growing acceptance of the balanced truth, which is that along with man's shadow side, his dark character,

2. In his fine book on this theme, *The One Quest,* Claudio Naranjo has said, "This is a time when we are abandoning forms and searching for the essence that animates them, an essence which often lies hidden in the forms themselves." (New York: Viking Press, 1972, p. 26.)

there is a thrust toward health and wholeness. The inner Self, as Jung has so carefully documented, instinctively seeks maturity, growth, light, creativity, openness, honesty.

The difficulty we have today is in learning to trust that there is good within us. We have difficulty in accepting the fact that our intuitive selves may be more fundamentally truthful than our rational calculations. We are just beginning to trust our deeper selves again, and depth psychology and encounter experiences are helping us. Meditation helps us get in touch with the positive resources within the self, and increasing numbers of people are learning meditation methods from one of the many traditions that utilize it.

This basic shift opens the way to the possibility of finding God in the unconscious. So long as we believe that there is only evil in us, we will fear to look within. If we learn that we also have within us good, strength, inspiration, direction, and potential, then we may look more deeply and open ourselves also to the possibility of the God within. For beyond the Self is God. Within us is the image of God, the stamp of the divine. Jesus knew and felt that divine presence within every person, from beggar to whore. We are beginning to trust that we can rediscover that jewel which Jesus saw in us, that pearl of great price, and that is indeed good news.

For the truth is that we are acceptable. There is not only evil in us; there is good as well. When we are honest about both, we are fully human. We need not be perfect, only honest, open to what we really are. And we are not just selfish, carnal, animal, sinful. This return to a balanced view makes it possible for people to believe once again in themselves, to believe in their acceptability, their okayness. This affirmative view, this balanced view that includes the affirmation of man, opens the doors to trusting our emerging psychic aspects such as extrasensory perception. Trust begets trust and doors open.

Reclaiming the Body

The fourth mark of the new religious style is the reclaiming of the body as part of the human being. There is a refreshing tendency today to honor the body, which is not the same as worshiping the body. To give the body its due is to honor the body as the residence of the feelings as well as of the mind, as having rich resources that we desperately need in order to be whole.

The heresy that says human beings should "rise above" their bodily or animal natures and live as rational, intellectual creatures has brought our world to the brink of destruction. By becoming so completely intellectual, we have cut ourselves off from real feeling, honesty about what is really going on within us, and a healthy honoring of the physical and intuitive side of our natures. We have learned how to fly to the moon, but not how to love the neighbor who is different from us. We are just beginning to reclaim the rich reality of what it means to be persons with both mind *and* body.

This renewed or reclaimed truth means that new religious styles can include the body as a resource. We can once again dance, move, shout, laugh, and cheer as well as listen, think, and meditate. When the body is ignored and becomes glutted with unexpressed angers and fears, we cut ourselves off from the resources of strength and will needed to cope with fear and anger.

Among the important recent books dealing with this reclaiming of the body is, as stated earlier, James Lynwood Walker's *Body and Soul: Gestalt Therapy and Religious Experience.* Walker helps us see the difficulties we encounter in rejecting the body and the current movement toward reclaiming it. Alexander Lowen, who has developed bioenergetic analysis as a form of psychotherapy that works with the whole person, mind and body, has written a very important book, *Depression and the Body,* in which he connects faith and the body. He speaks of faith as a biological phenomenon:

> Faith is a quality of being: of being in touch with oneself, with life, and with the universe. It is a sense of belonging to one's community, to one's country, and to the earth. Above all it is the feeling of being grounded in one's body, in one's humanity, and in one's animal nature. It can be all of these things because it is a manifestation of life, an expression of the living force that unites all beings.[3]

It is incredible enough to find a psychoanalyst speaking of faith, but Lowen's insights on the relation between faith and the body are groundbreaking.

Let us rejoice that in our religion as in our life, we are beginning to reclaim joyously the richness of our body and of our whole selves. This return to the physical man does not mean that we reject or forget to use our intellect. The problem is simply that we have become too intellectual and left our physical selves behind. We must continue to use our minds now enriched with feelings and intuitive bodily wisdom. We urgently need both.

Variety of Needs

The fifth mark of the emerging religious style is the awareness that persons have differing needs in religious paths. Most religious institutions have a power complex. They really expect that every "good" member should worship in the same way all the others do, in the same place, at the same time, and under the same leader. But this ignores a basic fact of human existence

---

3. New York: Coward, McCann & Geoghegan, Inc., 1972, p. 219.

—namely, that human beings are different. Some persons find their religious life fed by silence or by solitary meditation. Others seem to come alive best, or to have been reborn, in a one-to-one relationship with a guide or spiritual director or psychoanalyst. Yet others find intensive small group experiences to be the most deeply religious experiences of their lives. There are also persons who prefer a collective form of religious expression such as the traditional Sunday services. And the list could go on.

Individual expression has not been encouraged by the massive religious groups. And so the person who found inspiration in other than the prescribed ways under the prescribed leadership has been discouraged, ridiculed, and even castigated. Yet why should everyone be expected to find religious inspiration in the same way? Why should everyone find sermons and responsive readings stimulating? With the options narrowed intolerably, little wonder that millions stay away. Many people then feel they are not interested in religion, whereas, in truth, they may be more spiritual than the religious leaders who have turned them off.

Happily, the new religious attitude says that it is all right to seek your own path, to find your own style of religious expression and nourishment. And your style may be, as mine is, a combination of all possible forms with little or no routine. I find Quaker silence feeds me at times. I meditate, yoga style or Zen style. I explore dreams and meditation fantasies and find God there. And at other times I go to church to hear the great music, to sing and pray in concert with others. I do not wish to be bound in deadening routine to any of these forms. That would be dreary to me, even while I recognize it is important for many others. The conformity norms encouraged or enforced by the great religious groups are simply unrealistic, foolish, and counterproductive. People will continue to turn away from such unrealistic attempts to program their religious life in the manner of the herd.

Jung has proposed, from his extensive observation of human beings, that there are four basic personality types. There are those who are basically thinking persons, in whom feelings, intuition, and the sensation or practical function are less important. Others are more prominently intuitive and so on. It may very well be that we need a variety of religious approaches for this reason alone. For some persons, *thinking about* their religious life and its meanings may be the primary or only avenue to God. For others an approach that stresses feelings may be essential. And these differences in human beings cut across cultural and racial groups. Not all blacks are feeling types or intuitive types. Not all middle-class whites are thinking types. Yet our religious groups have operated on some such underlying assumptions and offered one approach for all, with little tolerance for other approaches.

The new religious style simply does not accept the old assumptions. All persons do not learn, grow, and worship in the same way. Freshness, vitality, the avoidance of stale routines, and the honoring of the individual are emerging norms.

Finding God in Nature

The sixth mark, and the final one on my list, is the return to nature. For centuries there has been a strong antinature attitude in Christian leadership. Religious feelings belong in churches, and if one feels "religious" out of doors, he or she may mislead the congregation. Carried to extremes, the churches may be empty and people may be wandering the hills and the forests on Sundays searching for God. Some such underlying nonsense has led church leaders to reject the deeply religious awareness to be found in natural surroundings.

When we reflect on religious history, the great leaders all found God in the solitariness of nature. Moses and the burning bush, Elijah in his cave, Jesus' forty days in the wilderness, St. Francis—the list is a long one. And there is a growing tendency today to rediscover the incredible depth of a single flower or a magnificent tree and to feel the life vibrations in man's primeval connection with all of nature and all living matter.

Some of the deeply intuitive poets who sensed this relationship to nature were dismissed (intellectually) as pantheists, those who *worshiped* nature. I do not wish to worship nature. But to worship in and through nature is to feel the deep abiding presence of God in Creation. To walk in the Alps or the Rockies in the spring can be a deeply religious experience that renews my spirit, reaffirms my relationship to God and man, and prepares me to reenter the world of concrete and brick.

I have, on occasion, seen churches send their congregations out of doors on a beautiful day to find the countless expressions of God's presence just outside their very doors. But many still mistrust this as a religious experience. Interestingly, it is our scientists today, our ecologists, who are calling people to rediscover their deep and inescapable interrelationship with nature. We have ignored that relationship too long, and almost destroyed the life-giving environment that nourished us to life. The new religious style honors that relationship and provides opportunities to return to it, not just as outdoorsmen and women, but as persons who belong to that nature and draw strength from it even as we give to it.

It may be God's plan to withdraw his/her spirit from traditional religious institutions and let the world be the Church. More and more, as people are recognizing and admitting their deep spiritual nature, they are not putting denominational labels on their spirituality.

This breakdown of the traditional, this awakening of man's

spirituality, this movement toward more individual religion opens the way for the emergence of a new style—informal, spontaneous, personal, open—relating conscious and unconscious, body, mind, and spirit. It is the appearance of this new religion of consciousness that excites me and gives me hope for man in his return to faith.

74 75 76 77 10 9 8 7 6 5 4 3 2 1